D1546366

JUMP IN THE WAVES

JUMP
IN
THE WAVES

A MEMOIR

Jacqueline Piatigorsky

A
Joan
Kahn
BOOK

ST. MARTIN'S PRESS

New York

Grateful acknowledgment is made to Editions du
Seuil for permission to reprint *"Lorsque le Pelican,"*
a poem by Alfred de Musset from *Ouvres
Completes.*

Library of Congress Cataloging-in-Publication Data

Piatigorsky, Jacqueline.
    Jump in the waves : a memoir / by Jacqueline
  Piatigorsky.
      p.   cm.
    "A Joan Kahn book."
    ISBN 0–312–01834–7
    1. Piatigorsky, Jacqueline.   2. Piatgorsky, Gregor,
  1903–1976—Family.   3. United States—Biography.
  4. Paris (France)—Biography.   I. Title.
  CT275.P6A3   1988
  794.1'092'4—dc19
  [B]

                                          87–38242

                    "A Joan Kahn Book"
                    FIRST EDITION
              10   9   8   7   6   5   4   3   2   1

To Grisha's memory, to Jephta and Joram

My thanks to:

Florence Wasson without whose insistence this book would not have been written.

Virginia Briggs who encouraged and guided me in the early stages of this book.

Marilyn Sorel for translating from French what I wrote when I was eighteen years old and expertly integrating it into my manuscript.

Myra Livingston for her friendship, her encouragement, and help.

Adele Siegal for her time, her superb typing and editing.

Harriet F. Pilpel for her assistance.

Special thanks to my children Jephta and Joram for their support and their help.

And above all I am grateful to Eva La Salle Caram for her patience in working with me, for her sensitivity and kindness, for her editorial guidance, and for her extreme competence without which this book could not have been published.

With sad eyes, dark and scared, clutching a doll
In the palace I ran from Rembrandt to Van Moll.
Behind massive marble stairs I crumpled and hid
Over glistening billiard balls my fingers slid.
A creeping shadow through the spacious hall
I faded in search of blurred echo tones
Draped in Gobelins I stepped on precious stones
From heaps of silk and gold I sobbed a call
But for a bird, over damp lawns of green
My silent prayer for love remained unheard.
Under deeply rooted trees, I drifted and grew
Under monuments, power and life I was new
In ocean of splendor I was alone
Mud and laughter were for me unknown.

JACQUELINE PIATIGORSKY
Philadelphia, 1946

CONTENTS

I

Ptichka

[1]

Ptichka

Fear is the story of my life. Envy, ungratefulness, confusion filled my youth. Alone in the austerity of a palace, a "museum," I dreamt of success.

"Ptichka," which means little bird, is for everyone who feels small, vulnerable, crushable, without hope. But in me, beneath the little bird hid a drive to achieve a full life, a fight against becoming bitter, against being driven by hate and sinking into waste.

Eventually love filled my internal turmoil. I gave love and I received love, and through love became creative.

I was born a Rothschild, but growing up a Rothschild was not all happy. There is another side to the medal. My parents admired winners, so for many years I mistook winning for success. In time I discovered that success is an internal feeling of peace and satisfaction. If recognition becomes a goal, it fails. Success can only be the result of a hard struggle, of genuine love for and interest in one's activity.

I want to tell what it is like to be treated harshly as a little girl, what it means to face unfairness. "Ptichka," my husband said to me to express tenderness when I seemed fragile. But sometimes little birds do not awaken tenderness.

One of the first things I remember of my mother was connected with a little bird. We were sitting outside and a sparrow flew down on the lawn fairly close to us. My mother was frightened; she gasped and got up to run away.

"What is the matter?" I asked, bewildered.

"I don't like it. It flutters."

"But it's only a little bird."

My mother smiled and said nothing else.

Birds were to play an important part in my life. There was an aviary in Ferrières in which I spent time with the golden pheasants, the pink ibis, the *colombes poignardées*, small gray birds with a dash of red feathers on their chests, making them appear to have been stabbed by a dagger. I stood in front of a very large cage where several hundred parakeets flew en masse from one tree to another. Later, for many years I gazed out of my bedroom window and watched ducks and swans on a lake; and still later, when I became a teenager, I joined my father's hunting parties in Ferrières and took part in the killing of beautiful pheasants.

And finally, when I learned to express myself in art, I sculpted birds.

[2]

Not Belonging

I was born in luxury. My father was the head of the Rothschild Bank in Paris. I do not remember any contact with my mother and father when I was a young child, and from my early years remember only Nanny, my English nurse. I was isolated from my parents because the custom of the time for wealthy families was to entrust their children to nannies. As my parents' quarters were far from the nursery, visits to them seemed expeditions. We lived in Talleyrand's palace overlooking the Place de la Concorde and the Jardin des Tuileries. My great-grandfather, James, had purchased it from Prince Talleyrand's heirs shortly after his death; then gave it to his son, Alphonse, who bought so many great art pieces that our home could have been mistaken for a museum. My relationship with my mother was somewhat distorted because of the special circumstances surrounding my birth.

From all appearances I was privileged. When I was growing up, acquiring a profession was beyond even a dream: my father's voice still echoes in me saying, "Girls need not work." He meant that my happiness lay in becoming a good wife and a social butterfly. But my aims went far beyond what my parents had decided my life should be.

My mother was young and very beautiful; my father, tall, thin, with a mustache, was a gentleman in the real sense of the word, refined and nervous, with kind melting eyes. Until he

inherited the palace on rue St. Florentin he lived with my
mother in a large apartment in Paris. My father also became
the owner of several places in the country. The most important
of which was the Château de Ferrières in Ferrières-en-Brie, a
little village half an hour's drive from Paris, this magnificent
place, where in 1862 Baron and Baroness James received the
visit of the Emperor Napoleon III, was built in the 1850s on
land my great-grandfather James had bought from the heirs of
Fouché, the minister of Napoleon I. The architect retained was
the Englishman Joseph Paxton, famous as the creator of many
illustrious buildings, including the Crystal Palace in London.
He also designed the thousand-acre park around the château.
Ferrières was not my parents' only country place. They also
owned the Manoir Sans Souci in the suburb of the town of
Chantilly in the province of Oise where we spent several weeks
in the spring and in the fall. My father's extensive stables were
very close to where we lived and to an immense training field
for the racehorses called *Les Aigles*. My father bred and raised
racehorses, and in the fields of Meautry where the horses ran
freely, each mother was followed closely by her baby, a beautiful and touching sight. When the young horses were old
enough to race, they were transferred to Chantilly. Château
Lafite, with its famous vineyards, also belonged to my father
and still produces some of the best wines of France.

Before I was born, my mother, as a young married woman
barely out of her own restricted childhood, faced the world
with the glorious perspective of unlimited possibilities. She
could make any decision. She had no fears and believed nothing could go wrong. "No old grouchy nanny for my children,"
she asserted. So her two sons were entrusted to a charming
young English nurse, and my mother was happy. She indulged
in a flashy social life, ordering many new dresses and decorat-
ing them with beautiful jewelry. She fluttered from one party
to another and enjoyed it when men turned around to look at
her as she passed. One early fall day, the attractive young
baby-sitter came and told her that Phon-Phon, as he was nick-
named after his grandfather Alphonse, seemed to have an upset
stomach. "He threw up," she announced. "Ordinarily I
wouldn't think much of it but he has been sick on and off all
summer, so I thought I should tell you."

"How long has this been going on?"

"About three or four months."

"You should have told me sooner. I'll get a doctor."

The doctor diagnosed appendicitis as the cause of Phon-Phon's vomiting. In 1910 the operating techniques were not perfected, nor were the anesthetics. My parents set up an operating room in Ferrières which, of course, was not sterile, nor did it have the facilities of a hospital. I will never know for sure, but perhaps Phon-Phon died a few hours after the operation because chloroform was used instead of ether. He was four years old.

My mother came home from the funeral and said, "I want another child immediately." Nine months later I was born. I came to replace a neglected and lost son. I was loved with guilt. I was treasured with fear. My name was Jacqueline de Rothschild. Yes, I was a Rothschild, but a girl. Were my parents disappointed? I wondered.

After my mother realized she could not trust nice young baby-sitters, she returned to the old tradition of hiring experienced, frustrated "old maids," classical English nannies. My mother had found out that we had to be properly cared for. Safety had become overwhelmingly important.

This was in 1911 when mothers from wealthy families didn't care for their children themselves. If the nurse were well recommended, only her capacity to keep the child safe and under control mattered. Her character was never looked into. It was pure luck if she turned out to be kind.

When Phon-Phon died, a nurse called Miss Cass took charge of my brother Guy. Though he was only two, he felt the loss and when taken for a walk ran after every boy wearing a sailor suit, calling "Phon-Phon, Phon-Phon."

For some unknown reason, a second nurse, Miss Carden, was engaged when I was born. Maybe Miss Cass was not considered strong enough to handle two children, but as she had been good with my brother, my mother was encouraged to keep her. In any case, there were two nurses for two babies. Unfortunately, the two women were rivals and refused to see each other, keeping my brother and me apart.

I still remember one day when a man wearing white gloves announced, "Lunch is served." I ran down the hall into the dining room. My brother Guy, sitting beside his nurse, was already eating. The oblong table could easily seat twenty-five, but my brother and his nurse were alone. They turned toward me and remained silent. I stood in the middle of the room, my arms hanging awkwardly.

"Jacqueline, Jacqueline, what are you doing?" yelled a distant voice. I stared: did I not belong there? My brother glanced at his nurse. There was between them a silent agreement. They went on with their meal.

"Jacqueline!" repeated the voice. But I stood a little longer; I was afraid. What did I do? I wondered. There was no answer to that so I shrunk my head a little into my shoulders and retreated. I went down the corridor past the linen room where several women were sitting, and ran straight back to my nanny. "You know we don't eat with them," she said. Yes, I probably knew, but I wasn't even three years old; I didn't understand, and that was frightening.

"I wouldn't eat with them," I heard Miss Carden mumble. "No, not me, I wouldn't eat with them—I would not."

From the other side of the door I heard more complaints from maids in the linen room. One of them said, "Really, that is too much—those English women, two separate lunches . . ."

I turned toward the sound of the voice. She too was angry. What did I do? I once again wondered, and there was still no answer. I felt like crying. "Nanny," I called.

"Yes, darling?" she answered, but I remained silent. Miss Carden came to me with a kiss and asked, "What is the matter, dear?"

As I couldn't explain I said finally, "I want to go to the bathroom."

[3]

Art

The walls were covered with paintings. To me they were just pictures: a rearing horse by Velasquez, an older man studying a globe by Vermeer, a young girl with a white pigeon by Boucher, country scenes, portraits by Rembrandt and Holbein, a huge painting with a monster trying to kiss a half-naked young woman by Rubens. I saw them daily but paid no attention. I never stopped to look at them, but I lived with them and they became part of me. I didn't think they were "good"; I took them as much for granted as my picture books or the wallpaper. But without realizing it, quality soaked deep into my unconscious. I must have been eighteen when my parents stood in front of a small Monet, a boat scene, which was for sale. To my bewilderment, they were in ecstasy. My mother raved about its beauty. I looked and saw only boats. I wondered, Am I deficient or is my mother's admiration for Monet's fame rather than for the picture?

To my mother, music symbolized greatness and beauty. She took singing lessons, but I never heard her sing or even hum a tune. What she really got out of music I never knew. My sister Bethsabée and I were given piano lessons even though we had no natural ability for music. We had a few dance lessons which were basically exercises. Real dancing seemed to me out of reach, not an activity through which I could express myself, until one day (I might have been in my early teens) when I was taken to see Anna Pavlova. Suddenly a new world flashed into my life. Each movement of her body was full of magic. In "The Dying Swan" her arms didn't seem part of a human body. They quivered and fluttered like the wings of a wounded bird. I fell in love. I never mentioned it to anyone, but for a few weeks when I was alone in my room I tried desperately to get on my toes. Of course it wasn't possible and eventually I gave up trying, but it was the first time I had been deeply moved.

Though I don't remember where I had seen it, I liked the dynamic rhythm of tap dancing. I must have asked to learn how to tap because once a black man came to teach me. He came only once and I didn't learn from that single lesson, though many times in years to come I tried to do what he showed me. Sometimes I try even now.

Though I was surrounded by great paintings, art, for me, had not yet come to life. It became approachable when I least expected it. In one of my yearly visits to her, I discovered that my grandmother painted. She was always sitting in an armchair and wearing a large dress that reached the floor. Such voluminous clothes made her seem fat, though I don't think she really was. I had never seen her out of that armchair and wondered if she really knew how to walk. One day in her living room a simple still-life was set up opposite her. A couple of apples, a vase and a knife sat awkwardly among knickknacks and a brocaded table cover.

"What is that?" I asked.

"I painted it," she said as she picked up a small canvas which had been leaning against her chair. I looked at the apples, the vase, the knife; they were all on the canvas. I was surprised and impressed. No one had told me about my grandmother's talent. Maybe painting was not a fashionable activity; my mother ignored it as an unimportant pastime. I looked at the little canvas, then at my grandmother, and asked, "Did you really do that?"

Encouraged by my interest, she actually got up and offered to show me her studio. She walked with a cane, slowly, in pain. She had arthritis in her hip, and in that era the recommended treatment was immobilization. I was in the studio for a short while and just stood, impressed by its simplicity. I saw an easel, a few canvases, and a wonderful light. Neither my grandmother nor I spoke and the studio was quiet; the quietness reflected peace and almost quivered, as if pointing to some future activity. In that moment I realized that my grandmother was not living in a museum as we were at home. She was surrounded not by famous paintings but by photos and paintings *she* had created. For the first time I saw painting as a simple re-creation of real life. A flash went through my mind; could *I* do that?

Though I saw my grandmother too seldom to have much of an exchange with her, I think she must have been an interesting person. She loved to entertain. Once a week she held what she called "literary luncheons." Among her friends were famous poets and personalities of the era, such as Madame de Noialles and the poet Paul Valéry. When I was seventeen I attended one of those luncheons and marveled at Madame de Noialles' capacity to talk. Sparkling with wit, she needed no conversational help, and her delighted listeners seldom interfered. Grandmother Halphen visited Ferrières once a year but stayed only two or three days, and I saw so little of her that I had to be reminded to go to her room for a good morning greeting on the way out. Later I wondered why there had been such an absence of family warmth toward her, why visiting her was a duty. Maybe because when my father proposed marriage to my mother he was refused at first. My grandmother was hoping her daughters would not marry Jews. It was the end of the era of the *Affaire Dreyfus*, which had stirred up considerable anti-Semitism. She succeeded in getting her second daughter, my aunt Alice, to marry into the French aristocracy, and her marriage was miserable.

The lack of warmth toward my grandmother could also have been a reaction to her strong, domineering character; my mother had struggled to escape her power. After my mother was supported by my father's position she developed her own power, so when my grandmother entered the family she seemed to me like a dictator in exile. In spite of that situation, and although I did not know it at the time, with her modest ability for painting she had planted a seed in me which took twenty-five years to come alive.

[4]

Meeting My Sister

When I was three, at the beginning of World War I, my sister was born and a third nurse was engaged. I remember entering the gardens of the Champs Élysées, walking beside my nurse. "Oh, look who's coming!" said Miss Carden. I saw a red-faced matron, a stranger, pushing a perambulator. As my nurse seemed pleased with the meeting, I ran toward the carriage and tried to peep in. At that moment a boy I knew to be my brother came skipping up from another direction. "Oh, what a coincidence," said Miss Carden. I looked at Guy. Yes, it was he with whom Nanny would not have lunch. He came up to the carriage and also tried to see. I was lifted, and though I stared deep into the dark hood I saw nothing.

"Did you see the little baby?"

"Yes," I lied, still wondering what was in the carriage.

"That sweet little baby is your sister." A baby! I suddenly wanted to look again to see it, to touch it, to love it. My baby! But the carriage had gone by and I stared at the back of the British matron.

I felt that an important event had entered my life . . . but what was it? The name sister meant nothing to me. I wanted to ask, "Is it really a baby? Is it really my baby? Can I look again?" But I didn't dare; I had lied about seeing her.

Frustrated, bewildered, head down, I walked in silence. Twice a day those walks were sacred; no matter if it was cold, hot, drizzling, or even raining, the nannies considered fresh air important. I wondered if I would see "my baby" again.

[5]

What to Ask

Even after a few years had gone by, the tragedy of my brother Phon-Phon's death was still discussed and left a heavy sadness in the air.

We were in Ferrières, walking down a large alley. I must have been quite young, as I remember Nanny was pushing a perambulator and talking to someone, and as I walked beside her holding the bar my head didn't reach the handle. The alley was uneven, with some muddy spots between the gravel. The sun barely penetrated through the leaves of many chestnut trees, and these heavily loaded trees strew the ground with their fruit: small, round green shells covered with thin spikes, many of them split open, revealing a little of their hidden treasure, shiny golden brown chestnuts. I picked them from the ground, caressing their slippery, silky covers.

My brother ran ahead; Nanny was talking low and there was a strange secrecy in the air. "What did you say?" I asked.

"Nothing . . . nothing, why don't you go and play?" This was thrown at me with just enough haste to increase my curiosity.

"What are you talking about?"

"Nothing, run along . . ." Turning to Miss Cass, Nanny mumbled, "We shouldn't speak in front of the children." Turning back to me, she said, "Little girls don't question like that. Run and play." Her words were final. The door seemed to slam in my face. I was kept out. But out of what? I looked up at my two guardians and they seemed embarrassed. I looked around. We had reached an open circle, the meeting point of several alleys. In the center a little round pond remained empty. The aged stone partly covered with moss stood colorless and seemed to add a nostalgic atmosphere to the unknown world around me. Catching up with my brother, I asked, "What is it?"

"What is what?"

"I don't know—there is something—I don't know." He didn't bother to answer, and I didn't know what to ask. I felt so much and knew so little. I looked down as I kept on walking silently. I picked up a chestnut and another, a light brown one, a darker one. I held them as I went. I felt part of a whispered sadness, and fear was part of me.

The park extended; I saw a clearing, a lawn, a cedar tree, blue cedars, purple elms, pines, oak trees, a lake, a red brick bridge on one side, a white iron one on the other, corners with tall grass, sun, space, moisture, a castle squarely shaped by four towers, a large main alley from the castle to the outer farm, a zoo, a golf course, small alleys, a large Greek marble sculpture, trails—every corner was cared for. The park was alive with rabbits, hares, moles, hedgehogs and weasels, pheasants and deer. Men were very scarce. Once in a great while a gardener would walk by or ride a bicycle past us, moving silently and peacefully, a live shadow of efficiency. Cut wood and hay spread a delicate fragrance in the air. Even the atmosphere with its soft light seemed aged and ageless. I was part of movement and stillness, silence that spread, silence that penetrated, silence that rippled and turned to life. Within the infinity of this enclosure I loved and feared.

[6]

Withholding

Three nurses for three children parading and smothering their little possessions seemed cumbersome, so my brother and I were reunited with my newborn sister under the care of the red-faced matron, Miss Swainston, our nanny, under whose power I would remain until I was sixteen years old. My first recollection of Nanny is her asking, "Who wants to pay a visit?"

"I do!" said my brother.

I immediately challenged him, "I do too!"

"Me first."

"No, me first."

We were fighting over some unknown destination. I was filled with the expectation of pleasure. Though young, I was strongly convincing. I had to go first. So I won my first important victory. "Go ahead," said Nanny. I looked somewhat bewildered. "If you need it so badly, go ahead," she repeated, pointing to the toilet. I walked in silently, closed the door, and sat. After a while her menacing words came to me: "What on earth are you doing? You were in such a hurry!"

I couldn't do anything so I sat, searching for a way out. I was again shrieked at. In desperation, I had to save face, so I flushed the toilet and answered, "I finished." I was humiliated and scared, and a liar.

Soon after, as the storm cleared, I really needed to go and

"pay a visit" but there was no way to explain, so at three years
of age I learned to withhold. I was starting a long career of
internal tumult; I became quite expert in withholding. Tension
grew as I became more and more aware of the urge and increased the concentration on my body. Fear of an accident intermingled with the pleasure of an almost sensual anxiety.
Satisfaction and panic gripped me as the first few drops
moistened my pants. I ran to the bathroom only when my
clothes were quite wet. From that day I always waited when I
needed to go to the bathroom. Maybe I was too proud to go to
Miss Swainston and ask, or maybe I was afraid that when
awarded the permission I would be unable to accomplish my
mission, or maybe the pleasure and torment of withholding
was secretly exciting. I never knew. Of course, I got scolded
each time I wet my pants. "You are dirty, don't do that!"
Nanny said. As insults and punishments did not seem to affect
me, she tried slapping me; then one day she rubbed my nose in
the wet pants. Nothing helped.

Sometimes I wondered why our previous guardians had left
and where they had gone. But as we were never spoken to as
thinking individuals, I developed the habit of taking things for
granted. I never learned how to question what happened
around me or even what I saw; consequently, I developed an
immense apathy for thought. I didn't express my feelings with
moods and my desires didn't burst out with tantrums. They
were kept within, but I was passionate so I soon became confused with contradictory emotions which often produced vio-
lent headaches.

Yes, we did have a mother and a father but their apartment
in the same palace was so far away that it seemed in a different
city. Our quarters, the nursery, consisted of two bedrooms—
one for my brother and the other for Nanny, my sister Bethsabée, and myself—a schoolroom for Bethsabée and me, a separate one for Guy, an extra room and a large dining room. This
apartment on the right side of a long corridor overlooked the
Obélisque, surrounded by fountains on the Place de la Concorde, and children playing with toy boats on a little pond in
the Jardin des Tuileries. The toilet room looked on the rue St.
Florentin, a narrow street. Directly across stood the Ministère

de la Marine in which a young sailor sometimes looked out of the window directly across from the toilet room, faced me, and smiled.

On each visit to the bathroom, I first looked to see if he was at the window. Before I retired to "pay a visit" I was glad when he was there to exchange a smile. A few years later when I got my first dog, I held it up and showed it to my unknown sailor friend. He lifted his arms, adding surprise to his smile.

Though I had become competent at withholding, my mastery was insufficient, and relying on my expertise led me to a very embarrassing experience.

I was eight or nine when my cousin Colette became my very good friend, my only friend, my only contact with the outside world. She was lively, quick, witty, daring. In Ferrières we bicycled, laughed, giggled, picked our noses, had sexual games, and gossiped. She told me once how, while playing hide-and-seek at some friend's home, she had hid on the roof and, when her friend was about to find her, jumped, escaping from her playmates. When in the air, she noticed that she was going to land on a glass roof. To her great relief, the glass did not break.

One day when Colette and I were staring at the swans' harmonious glide, making noiseless ripples on the lake, I thought of Nanny's rigid discipline, butlers and footmen serving me. Where could I find adventure? Colette helped me. Her advice was: "All you need is guts. The other day my brother Gilbert locked the big glass door and sneered at me. I told him that if he didn't open immediately I would go through anyway. He stood and dared me."

"So what did you do?" I asked, vibrating as if challenged myself.

"I turned sideways," she proudly announced, "and hit the door with my shoulder. The glass crashed. Bleeding, I calmly walked past him."

One day she invited me and several other children to her house. As I never went out, I felt shy and very uneasy. I didn't know how to cope with a group, so I remained quite silent, wishing it were time to leave. At lunch we were all sitting around the table where her mother was also present. While two footmen served, I suddenly felt an urge to go to the bathroom. Of course I held back. As holding back had become routine, I was overconfident and in spite of my experience, and to my great surprise, I let out a big "noise." Every face reddened as a heavy silence spread. A voice broke the tension: "It wasn't me!"

Then another, "It wasn't me!"

Then another and another, "Not me" . . . "Not me."

My heart pounded as my turn came. All I had to say was "Not me," but guilt and embarrassment paralyzed me. It was me. Lie, I thought, trying to encourage myself, you have lied before. Just say it, "not me." But I couldn't and remained silent as all eyes turned to me, waiting. Colette's mother repressed a sarcastic giggle and spoke of something else.

[7]

A Win, Not a Success

O nce I won an important victory that turned to failure.

My sister and I were to be vaccinated. We both stared intensely at the cotton wool, the alcohol, the knife. I asked no questions, put up no fight, just stood, my heart pounding. "Whoever doesn't cry," said Nanny, "will get a candy." And all at once the preparations seemed less forbidding. A ray of hope, something to win. I was proud and full of a desire to be stoic. I told myself, "Don't cry when the knife cuts and you earn a candy." Finally I faced a real challenge; I could make a tangible effort and expect a concrete reward. Even more, I had a chance to dominate. I glanced at my sister, the baby Nanny loved. "Me first!" I ventured, stepping forward. Because of my passionate nature, I was happy to have something to compete for. Maybe Nanny would look up to me; also, maybe she would even love me. I watched with perfect quietness as the knife lacerated my skin.

"Good," said the doctor as he turned to my sister. I became nervous. Would she cry?

Yes, tears rolled down her cheeks as he took hold of her ankle. Then she lost all control and screamed. I had won. Ready to triumph, I stood expectantly. As my sister continued to cry even though the operation was quite over, Nanny picked her up, hugging her with tenderness. "It is all right, darling; it is all over." I felt clumsy, gazing at a world of love I could not penetrate. As I leaned against the wall and waited, I felt small and defeated even though I had won. Remembering my victory, I walked straight up to Nanny and asked, "Where is my candy?"

Nanny looked at her watch. "It's too close to dinner time," she said, "you will get it later." Disappointed but knowing the uselessness of arguing, I lowered my head. After all, what difference if I had to wait a little, there was still something to look forward to. But didn't we often have candy at bedtime? Was my win weakened?

After dinner, Nanny came with a candy. Yes, I had earned a candy only two hours ago. But it seemed as if it had been in a different life. With a faint smile I watched her come toward me. But she handed the candy to my sister, my rival. Turning to me, she said, as she often did, seemingly without reason, "You were bad, so you cannot get a candy tonight."

And that is how I experienced my second victory.

[8]

A Crushed Rebellion

"**G**o down and see your mother," said Nanny. "Don't be late coming up. It's already four-thirty; be here at five." So I went for my daily visit in the drawing room. My mother always dressed with elegance, in good taste, never showy. This evening she had a guest and I looked at the soft waves in Mother's hair surrounding the beautiful oval of her face.

But twenty minutes seemed endless with nothing to do. I fidgeted, asked the time, tried a question. Apparently, my mother found me a nuisance and, not knowing how to keep me busy, gave me a pencil and pad. Pointing to a large Gainsborough painting, she ordered, "Draw that." I looked at the painting and tried. My mother and her guest laughed. That I should be able to copy a painting was so unreal to my mother that it was funny. Yes, they laughed at me. Though I was very young, today I can still feel the sting of their laughter.

I had to be back in the nursery by five. "Don't be late," were Nanny's orders. "What time is it?" I asked every few minutes, till finally Mother answered, "Five o'clock." I barely said goodbye, dashed out, ran through the long halls, up the stairs, in and out of corridors, out of breath, straight to Nanny.

"You are late," she grumbled.

"Oh, no! I asked . . . I kept asking the time."

"Don't contradict me when I say you're late."

Protest started bubbling in me as I twisted my body.

"Don't turn your back to me like that!"

I stopped, defiantly hitting a chair with the tip of my foot. My stubbornness stirred her anger. She tore my clothes off and, grabbing me by both arms, dumped me in the bathtub with a splash. "Wash yourself," she ordered. Tears started rolling down my cheeks. "Don't sniffle, you're a disobedient child." I cried louder. "I will make you stop," she yelled.

She lifted me out of the tub, unwashed. I stood naked and dripping, screaming, my nose running fiercely. "You stop this very instant." Controlled, her voice had taken a menacing authority. But my rage was bordering on hysterics. She put a towel over my head and held it tight. "*Now* will you stop?"

"No," I yelled, stamping my feet and dribbling in spite of the towel over my face. "No . . . no . . . no . . ."

"All right, then, you can stay like that." She took a pin and fixed the towel, leaving me in the dark with a feeling of not enough air.

"Take it off," I screamed. "Take it off."

She let me wait, then said, "Now will you shut up! You are a bad child."

"Take it off," I repeated, still yelling.

"No. You won't stop? Then keep it on."

"I'll be good! Take it off, please take it off. I'll be good, I will be good. Please Nanny, take it off."

Released, I remained very quiet. My little sister Bethsabée had kept out of the scene. The nurse went to her and without any apparent reason picked her up and kissed her passionately. "*You* are my little darling," she said.

When Mother came up an hour later to kiss the children good night there was order and peace in the nursery. Miss Swainston, with a sweet smile, pushed forward an armchair for Mother to sit down.

From Withholding to Competing

One morning when I was six years old I entered the schoolroom with such an effort that it was difficult for me to walk from one room to the other. I couldn't sit straight, and my mind seemed even more empty than usual. But this was not uncommon, as I always stared at the books without ever getting involved. This day, however, seemed endlessly heavy. Voices, demands, reproaches echoed around me. I heard, "Pay attention . . . look what you're doing . . . eat your lunch . . ." I was dragging, my limbs were a weight, not part of my body. Finally night came.

The next morning I felt even worse. Nanny dressed me to go to the schoolroom. But finally, sensing something was wrong, she said, "Come here . . ." and put her hand on my burning forehead. I had over 104 degrees of fever. "Go to bed," Nanny said, and as I collapsed in bed I felt an immense relief. I was no longer bad, stupid, lazy. I would be comfortable in bed, and even be liked.

But days went by and I was still in bed, restless, with high fever. Doctors came and left. My room was kept in semi-darkness; I had special nurses, one for the day and a different one for the night. Weeks went by and I was still very sick. One night there were several doctors looking at me, then conferring in the next room. I sensed a crisis.

Of course I didn't know that I had peritonitis when the following morning I overheard, "There will be no need to operate;

the abscess has burst alone—it will drain by itself." From then on I started to feel better, but the days seemed longer and longer as I lay in bed. I twisted and turned and called the nurse, but there was nothing to do. Boredom was reaching a dangerous level when one morning a new nurse entered. "My name is Miss Coque," she said, "tomorrow I will bring you something."

"Oh, what?" I asked.

"You will see. It is a surprise. The only thing I can tell you is that with it you will never be bored again."

A surprise for me! I looked at her, not knowing what she meant. That night I slept well. And the next morning, barely awake, I asked, "Where is Miss Coque?"

"It is too early," I was told, "she will be in later." So I waited. Every few minutes I asked, "Is Miss Coque here? When will she arrive?" Then she really did arrive. The night nurse greeted her, saying, "Jacqueline has been asking for you." Miss Coque smiled and said nothing. I just looked at her and waited. She hung her coat, spoke to the night nurse, read some papers. I started to doubt that she really had something for me. But I thought it was nice to have her around anyhow. When finally we were alone she came to me, took a chair, and sat near the bed. Then she pulled out of her large pocketbook a small board. She opened a box containing little wooden pieces, placed them on the board and explained, "This is the king and this is the queen, the knight, the rook, the pawns. Look, this moves this way, that goes there. If you put this here it can take that one off." And suddenly I found myself moving the pieces, capturing hers, putting them back so they faced each other equally. I played with Miss Coque all day. I could not part with my new game. She was having fun too, which made the game even more thrilling. We played for hours. And suddenly the days went by quickly. I was surprised when I was told one morning, "Today you will get up." I had been in bed for several weeks and when I stood up my legs buckled under me. But soon strength came back and Miss Coque said, "You won't need me anymore; you're well now." My stomach turned into an empty pit. "You can keep the chess set," she went on, "it's yours. Good-bye, dear, and good luck to you." She left me with Nanny and soon I was thrown back into the old routine.

Yes, the chess set was mine and I treasured it. But it lay dormant in its box. A new life was bubbling in me; I yearned to play, but there was no one to play with. One evening my father said, "I'll play you a game." I jumped up to get the set and set up the pieces. "I haven't played for a long time," he said, "but I'll try." After a couple of games he started playing slowly. It was his move and he was sitting and thinking. He didn't seem able to move. I couldn't understand. I was just pushing pieces and he was suffering. He tapped his fingers on the table, humming some monotonous little rhythm. "Well," I said, "it's your move." I was getting annoyed. He waited still longer and finally moved. Although he had studied the position for such a long time, he left a knight where it could be taken. I grabbed the knight. "Oh, no! I didn't see it," he said, "I told you I hadn't played in a long time. I can't do it anymore." He got up and left.

I had won. But my father had walked off. He'd turned away from chess, from me. I sat alone in front of the chess board, frustrated, wanting to call to him, "Come back! Play some more." But he'd left.

Now chess had become more than a game, more than a companion. It had created an exchange with my father. We had actually competed, and I'd tasted a win. But more important even than the win was my feeling for chess: I loved the game, the pieces, how they moved, the challenge to find a solution to the infinite combinations. I had actually fallen in love.

The next day I asked my father to play but he wouldn't. Of course I hadn't liked the hours he seemed to take before making his move, but in spite of them I wanted to play. "No," he answered, "I have no time." But I kept on asking.

"I'm too old," he said, "I can't anymore." So, finally, I understood that he wouldn't play with me anymore and the pieces with their burning life went back into the box. But I couldn't let the game die. What to do? It didn't take me long to find a solution. I taught my four-year-old sister how chess pieces moved, and we played together—just the two of us. We didn't know the existence of books on chess, nor did we know that chess could become a study, but we found combinations. We didn't miss not knowing anyone else who played. We just played together—literally millions of games. Passionately involved, we played, fighting over blunders taken back. Being older, I had an edge over my sister and won more often than she did. The board and its pieces became part of our life, part of us. We kept discovering more combinations, but we played fast, without concentration or any thought to improving our game. Playing chess was our recreation, our pastime, our fun, and it became an important tool in our fierce competition. One day—I might have been in my teens—in Ferrières during a weekend hunting party my father called me. "Go and get your chessboard," he ordered, pointing at Jacques de Breteuil, one of my parents' friends who spent most weekends in Ferrières to join the hunting parties. "He wants to play with you." My opponent was a huge man weighing several hundred pounds. He had thick hands, covered with fat, and his enormous belly made his arms seem short. But in spite of his size he wasn't clumsy. His deep voice penetrated and he waddled around with a large voluptuous smile. As we sat down in the living room among all the other guests and faced each other across a small chessboard, I remained very silent. As it served to hide a little uneasiness, his smile now could almost be heard.

"She's good," said my father, pointing at me. "She'll beat you." And suddenly I felt worried. I wanted to protest, but I couldn't talk. Why did he say that? I had never faced anyone but my sister. I was on the spot, flustered and annoyed. As the game progressed my position became more and more difficult. My opponent's relief could be felt again through his smile. It was more reserved but soaked with a sadistic beam of triumph, like a baba bloated with rum.

I played on for a little while longer. Then I had to admit defeat. I had lost. My obese opponent got up and his smile flourished, accompanied by a faint cackle. My father ran up to me, casting a condescending glance. I said good-bye and left the room. I remained quiet and polite. But although I may have looked indifferent, inside I was devastated. I hadn't lived up to my father's proclamation. I had disappointed him. His daughter was not a genius. But what, I asked myself, gave him the right to make such a presentation? I was ashamed and angry, ashamed of myself, ashamed to face him. Deep in me a growing force needed revenge. I wanted to crush the world. "Some day," I murmured, "some day I'll show them!"

[10]

Repressed and Rewarded

Every summer we packed and moved to the seashore. Many suitcases were set out and a couple of big, heavy trunks. Nanny had two maids to serve her.

Once again it was summertime and the entire household—the cook and a boy to help him, the butler, footman, chauffeur, Nanny and two maids—were mobilized to transport two little girls to the beach a few hours' drive from Paris. The commotion and the work were done behind closed doors. We sensed complicated arrangements but we weren't part of them. Our routine was constant until we were stuffed into a car; then our duty was to sit very quietly until we reached the summer home.

The next morning we wore light clothes and went to the beach, where Nanny immediately rented a large tent and settled in just off the boardwalk in the fine sand. This, of course, was a change from our daily walks up and down the Champs Élysées. We were allowed to remain barefoot, and when we stepped on the sand we liked that warm, pleasant sensation. We dug our hands in the fine sand, letting it sieve through our fingers. We looked at the ocean but we weren't allowed to go close enough to it to get wet. Other children came and scattered all over, and soon the beach was covered with people, with boys and girls of all ages. Some of them ran with balls; some, with their feet in the waves, jumped and yelled. Many swam and others dug puddles or mud castles; the creative groups built an animal or a man or a village in the hard sand. But my sister and I, in the midst of so much life, were isolated. Some invisible fence seemed to hold us within a few feet of Nanny and her tent. We sat for a while just gazing, but Nanny knew that soon we would look for something to do. So she protected herself in advance: "Here is a shovel for each of you— dig," she ordered. We got up and slowly started shoveling sand. But it seemed senseless and we kept glancing at the children in the water. They were having such fun! "I told you to dig," repeated Nanny. The sun was hot and the light was strong. I suddenly felt tired, so I turned to Nanny and asked, "Can I go down to the water?"

"No!" She hurled the word at me. "Do as I tell you—dig." My sister didn't look up. She tried pushing sand around. I stood for a few seconds, then drew a large circle in the sand and started digging a hole. Drops of sweat were dripping down my back. The water seemed so cool. I stared from a distance at the waves gently coming and going. Craving to go down and touch them started to make my limbs ache. "Why can't I go to the water?" I asked again.

"Because I say so."

"But *why*?" I insisted.

"Don't ask stupid questions," she snapped, "just do as I say."

Revolt tried to bud its way through. I defied her: "I don't want to dig—I'm too hot."

"You're a bad, disobedient girl." Nanny was angry and her voice threatened. I looked down. "Go and play with your sister; she's good."

Nothing had changed since last year and the year before. I knew there was no breaking loose. I picked up my shovel again. The large circle I had made became smaller as the hole became deeper. I had reached below the fine sand and was building a wall around my hole. With each shovelful of sand, I was throwing out part of Nanny. After a while I was deep in the sand; I had to build a couple of steps so I could get in and out of my hole without damaging the walls. I could not see outside anymore and Nanny could not see me either. I paused for a few minutes, leaning against the side of my construction. From physical exertion and much sweating, I had rid myself of anger. I could stop digging without being nagged. I was alone. I had built my castle deep down, away from the world. I felt good. I could see no more children jumping in and out of the water. I could hear no more shouting and running. There were before me no more waves with their hypnotic back-and-forth pull, but only a monotonous, distant sound. As I patted the walls of my new home, protected by thick walls of sand, I felt suddenly free; the sand felt cold and hard—I had a home which I had built, a home where I could be good.

Effort is generally rewarded. Even though I had been forced to dig, the effort I made in creating a deep hole was well rewarded.

A surprise waited for me in my new home.

The hot sun was drying the sand and a little dribbled to the bottom. I immediately threw it outside, lifting the shovel above my head. As the metal cut clean wedges at the bottom of the floor, I noticed moisture appearing from nowhere and then immediately vanishing. I made balls, shoving them from one hand to the other until the sand was dry and crumbled. Suddenly I understood. I had found water. No effort could have been better rewarded. I called my sister. "Come here," I shouted. "Come here—quick!" She came and tried to join me, but the steps were too low for her to reach, so she half-jumped, collapsing a heap of sand with her.

"Look out, you fool, you are ruining everything," I shouted.

"What do you want?" she asked.

"Dig out the sand you brought down," I ordered.

"No," she said, "why should I?"

"Because I have something to show you." She looked at me but didn't move. I started to repair the damage. She helped me and we forgot to fight. "Look," I said, "if we dig far enough we'll find water."

The water appeared to us as a real miracle. We dug our feet in the mud, then we splashed our hands. We picked up the sand and water dribbled down our arms and legs. Deep down in a prisonlike hole we had found freedom and a secret treasure.

A few days later when we came back to the beach, the tide

was extremely low. There were miles of hard, rippled, wet sand
before the ocean. This day my brother accompanied us. He had
friends and immediately joined them and ran on the wet sand.
They ran back and forth, splashed in little puddles, then ran
toward the ocean. I didn't think for a second—I just ran after
the other children. "Come back! Come back!" shouted a familiar voice. I stopped and remained still. I was also on the wet
hard sand. The ocean was completely still. People were walking far into it and the water came only to their knees. A little
farther out I saw small rocks covered with some very green
slimy algae and mussels; the water between the rocks seemed
like tiny little lakes. Some children were playing with a crab;
others were pushing a stick with a net on the end and were
picking up shrimps. "Come back!" shouted Miss Swainston.
"Don't you hear me? Come back!" I stood glued to the spot, as
if paralyzed. What have I done? I asked myself. Guy and his
friends were far ahead; Nanny was shouting behind. Suddenly
a hand gripped my arm, shook me, and dragged me toward the
tent.

"*Can't* I play with the others?" I asked.

"No, you stay here and play with your sister."

I flopped on the hot soft sand to sulk. I squirmed and made
the sand fly. "Don't do that," Nanny ordered. I ignored her.
"Dig," she ordered, pointing to the shovel. "You dig—right
now or . . ." I picked up the shovel and dug. But the ocean was
too far away; I found no water this time.

That evening before dinner my brother whispered, "I told
Mother that she wouldn't let you play." I looked at him, happy
and scared. "Father is very angry," he said. Later when my
father came up to the nursery I was already in bed. Nanny
became very sweet, offering him a chair, but he didn't thank
her or sit.

"I heard that you forbade the children to play." My heart
was pounding. Nanny mumbled something. "Don't answer me
back." His voice was loud and threatening. Nanny tried to
walk away from him but he went after her, screaming. I heard
more screaming from the other room, then a door slamming,
and then nothing. Embarrassment and fear had stunned the
nursery. I was afraid to turn in bed. How could I face Nanny! A

time went by, she opened the door, picked up something, straightened the chairs, closed a drawer, folded a towel; then, finally, she came to me, tucked me in and without a word gave me a kiss and turned out the light.

The next day as we got on the beach, Nanny said, "Go and play." I started walking very slowly toward the ocean with my head down. I wasn't called back so I kept on walking with an uneasy feeling that I was stealing something. As I reached the hard, wet sand I loved the ripples under my feet. I looked back; I was far from Nanny and the cabin. I looked at the ocean; children jumped and screamed. Waves rolled back and forth. I stood very still, as though some invisible strength within me said "No." I retreated. Very sad and wondering what had gone wrong, I sat on the warm, fine sand.

The following summer my mother hired a boat with a man to run it. It was large enough to seat a lot of people, but it was only for Nanny, my sister, and me. So instead of digging in the soft sand we went every morning for a ride on the ocean. I sat and gazed, at first bewildered by the light, the sparkle of the ocean, the changing colors.

The breeze catching the sail made the boat lean first on one side, and as we turned, on the other side. When there was no wind we sailed with a motor; then the boat went faster, cutting through the water, and I loved letting my hand hang over the side to feel the water as it splashed against the boat, throwing a fine spray. But after a while, just sitting and watching became monotonous. I wanted to do something. So I took my little chessboard and played chess with my sister, game after game, millions of games.

Miss Coque was so right in what she said when I was six years old: with a chess set, it was impossible to be bored.

[11]

Bethsabée

My sister was a thin baby with a round face, a mass of blond curly hair and blue eyes like my father and brother. I had long fluffy brown hair and brown eyes. I was brought into the world to replace Phon-Phon and I was the only one to have his coloring.

My little sister was almost four years old and she wouldn't walk. Nanny put her on her feet, held her hands and coaxed her, but she only stood for a few seconds, then plumped down and sat and played happily. I sensed my parents' and even Nanny's concern that she was so slow in learning to walk, but soon their worries increased: she wouldn't eat either. At eighteen months of age she had been operated on and had her appendix removed. Nanny would say, "Since the operation she won't eat," and that was the accepted reason for her refusal to eat. But why wouldn't she walk? they wondered.

For me she was more than a threat; she was a real danger, because Nanny loved *her* and not me. Why did Nanny have such a preference? Perhaps because Bethsabée was difficult, therefore a challenge, or perhaps because Nanny had nursed her since the day she was born and didn't begin taking care of me until I was three years old. But my feelings toward Bethsabée were mixed: she was my rival, but at the same time she was "my baby" and my friend against Nanny. I wanted her to walk, so I started trying to help her do it when no one was in the room. One day in Ferrières we were alone in the bedroom and I spoke to her. She seemed to be hesitating. I took her hand. She got up. "Walk," I ordered, "come on, walk." Maybe I was convincing and she wanted to please me, or maybe it was a coincidence, but she let go of my hand and walked. "Nanny!" I screamed, "come and see, she can walk." Bethsabée was still standing as Nanny entered.

"Well, darling, show me what you can do." She was hoping. I remained quiet, held my breath with pride, as I had already tasted success. Bethsabée hesitated for a second, then her legs buckled under her and she collapsed.

"Come on," I whispered, "get up, show her, walk." But she sat on the floor, smiled, and said nothing. Nanny turned to me. "You always lie," she said.

"No, she did walk—she really did—she did."

Miss Swainston hesitated. "What did you do?"

"Nothing, I did nothing—she just walked."

"Nonsense, it is all nonsense," she said and left the room. When we were alone Bethsabée walked again, but this time I said nothing. Little by little she got stronger and eventually walked in front of Nanny.

"You see," I ventured, "I *told* you she could walk." But by that time Bethsabée's ability to walk was taken for granted and "our" achievement was engulfed in a daily routine. But my sister and I had become a little closer.

She still wouldn't eat, and I wasn't allowed to eat everything, due to eczema behind my ears, a common skin irritation with tense children. But instead of understanding how difficult life was for me under Nanny's care, the doctors attributed my condition to various foods: chocolate, eggs, and sardines, all of which became forbidden. On the other hand, everything was tried to make my sister's dishes more tempting. Still she refused to eat, and I sat aching with envy as her plates remained full. So after breakfast I often managed to sneak back into the dining room before the table was cleared, and finish what Bethsabée had rejected. My biggest favorite was bread and butter fingers dipped in a soft-boiled egg. The craving for eggs has remained with me all my life. Years later, when I was married and free, I had an egg every morning for breakfast until

my doctor stopped me: too much cholesterol, she said; but I
still crave eggs. In the nursery Nanny tried begging Bethsabée
to eat. She tried distracting her, bribing her, then finally got
angry. But that only brought on tears and then Nanny would
give up. "Who ever heard of operating on an eighteen-month-
old baby—it is absurd," she would mumble, happy to have an
excuse for her failure. Then, pacified, she would pick up my
sniffling little sister and kiss her. "Poor little darling, what did
they do to you? Try this—no, you have to drink your milk. We
just won't leave the table until you drink it." And eventually
Bethsabée swallowed a cup of milk and nibbled on her bread
as so-tempting open sandwiches remained on her plate.

Even at that young age I had an unusual insight into the
reasons for my sister's behavior. Nanny had no understanding
of children, no patience, no kindness. Possibly, she had a sadistic streak that came through even in her apparent love for my
sister. By refusing to eat and walk Bethsabée unconsciously re-
belled; unfortunately she was destroying herself. Living under
the same terroristic power, it was easy for me to know that
Bethsabée's refusal of food had nothing to do with an operation
that she had no recollection of anyhow; I also intuitively knew
that many times she had to fight herself to be able to resist the
tempting little dishes before her. "Go ahead, eat it," I said,
trying to help. After all, I had made her walk.

"No."

"Change your mind; it's no disgrace," I explained.

"No," she repeated.

"But it will not be like giving in to Nanny. Eat it for yourself—I know you want it."

"No, I don't, I won't eat it."

She was acting like a mule and I couldn't break through. But
I made a last effort.

"At least taste it. It looks good."

Though I sincerely wanted to help her, part of me hoped the
food would remain on the plate so I could get a chance to steal
some while it was around.

Later my mother would ask, "Did she eat?"

"Yes, she ate a little." My mother was relieved. She felt safe
as long as Miss Swainston was with us. Little did she realize

that her precious Miss Swainston was the cause of my eczema, and of all Bethsabée's problems.

After a few years my sister developed a rachitic condition as the result of an insufficient diet. To correct it she was given a corset attached to a leather necklace by a metal stick. It looked very uncomfortable. To strengthen my sister's weak spine the doctors recommended sun baths in the mountains. Not having seen snow I got excited at the prospect of going with her.

"Will there be snow?" I asked.

"Yes, probably."

I started counting the days.

My nose was glued to the window as the train slowly curved up the mountain. "No snow," I remarked sadly.

"Maybe we are not high enough yet," I was told. I had been given false hope: we had nearly arrived and passed only one or two small patches of snow. I was bitterly disappointed. "Well, I guess it is too late in the season," Nanny said.

Our rooms had a balcony and we took sun baths. The first day we were exposed three minutes. I could not understand what the purpose was. It seemed especially absurd to count the minutes. How could such a short time have any effect? Every day the time was increased with the utmost care, and after a few weeks we returned with nice brown bodies. Maybe those sun baths were good for my sister but they were not much fun for me.

In Paris my sister and I slept in the same room. Miss Swainston's bed was in the center of the wall and we were on each side of her in the corners. We were dressed alike and we saw the same people. We had meals together, walks together, lessons together; we played together, we suffered together, we fought and hated each other. But, as if part of us was fused together, we also felt and understood each other. Between us, words became hardly necessary. Though we spoke enough, our words had become mumbling sounds. To anyone listening to us it might have seemed as if we had developed our own language.

In our bedroom there was a glass over the door. When the light went on we knew Nanny was close.

One night my sister said, "I don't feel like sleeping, I want to talk." Though I was tired, we chatted until I was half asleep and couldn't answer anymore. Suddenly the light went on.

"She's here; go to sleep," I whispered.

"I can't sleep," she said.

"Shut up, she'll hear us."

"I'll talk if I want to." Bethsabée spoke faster and louder, as if she wanted to be heard.

"Shut up, you idiot, shut up, she's coming, I hear her."

"I don't care; I'll tell her you won't let me sleep." The door opened. I lay motionless, my face toward the wall.

"What's going on?"

My sister blamed me, as she had announced she would. Miss Swainston came over to my bed. "You are not to talk. Go to sleep."

"It was her," I said, "I was half asleep—"

"Don't lie. You're the oldest; you should know better."

"I am not lying. It was not me, it was her."

"Don't always contradict." She sounded threatening. I turned and sat up, ready to defy. She slapped my face. "Be quiet," she ordered. "Lie down and go to sleep." She left the room and not another word was uttered.

The next day as we crossed a large street, Nanny, as usual between us, held our hands. I saw a car coming too fast. We almost had to run not to be hit. I turned around and gazed at the car coming down the street and I wished it would run over Bethsabée—I wished my sister were dead—I wished—I wished.

As time went by and we became adolescents, my sister and I, even though we had grown up in the same environment, developed differently. Bethsabée occasionally took advantage of her position, but mostly we were friends. I was the oldest, a double-edged position: between us I was the leading force. I had to dominate her person, her mind, her wishes, even her thoughts. I was so hungry to possess my little sister that I constantly asked, "What are you thinking of? What are you looking at?" Sometimes she would pretend to have a secret or some private fantasy. Then, possessed by a gnawing curiosity, I hounded her with questions until I found out. One day I asked, "Will you promise me something?"

"I don't know. What is it?"

"Promise and I will tell you."

"It depends, what?"

"I can't tell you until you promise." By then she thought I was withholding some important discovery and she knew that I would never give in. To save face she pretended to fight for her rights, but soon accepted. "I promise. Tell me what is it?"

"I want to know everything you are thinking. Promise to tell me everything you think."

"I can't do that."

"But you already promised."

"Everything I think!" She was weighing the enormity of what she had accepted.

"Yes, every thought that goes through your mind."

"Will you also tell me what *you* are thinking?" she asked.

"Maybe, whenever I can, but you promised! Can I trust you?" Finally she agreed with a total surrender and I felt satisfied.

[12]

Fear

I lived in fear from the first day Miss Swainston took charge of me. She made sure my sister and I were safe, but in the process she brutalized us with her harsh orders and her unfairness.

I had learned to deal with different kinds of fears. At three years of age the fear of wetting my pants had become a major issue. Later I knew the fear of returning late to the nursery; the fear of the unknown, when I sensed a mystery and did not know what to ask; the fear of long dark corridors; the fear of remote corners of the woods, when I bicycled alone in Ferrières; and the fear of being discovered when my friend Betty Hunter, the caretaker's daughter, and I bicycled around the park. And, still at sixteen, the fear of elevators.

We were to report to Nanny every twenty minutes. One day Betty said, "The concierge at the Pont-Carré gate has a sister working in the chocolate factory. If we ask her she will give us some chocolate bars." As this was far away, at the most distant point of the park, we rushed off. When we got to the gate the concierge really gave each of us one thick bar of solid chocolate. I ate mine with a sensuous passion. It was delicious, an overwhelming treat. At home all chocolate was forbidden, as it supposedly initiated the eczema which was pestering me. Out in the woods it seemed as though the luscious pure chocolate was filling my entire body with strength and sunshine. We

were already halfway back and I was still savoring the delicious sweetness of pure chocolate when a fear hit me.

"Will Nanny notice chocolate on my breath?"

"Of course not," Betty said.

"She will, she will. I can't go back. I just can't. But it is
nearly twenty minutes. Betty, what can I *do*?" I was gripped by
fear.

"I know." She sounded a little surprised. "We can stop at the
faisanderie and get a glass of water."

"Yes," I agreed. But we certainly had to hurry. We got back
almost in time, panting and dripping wet.

"What did you do?" asked Nanny.

"Nothing, nothing," I hurriedly told her, out of breath. "It's
far to go to Pont-Carré and back in twenty minutes." Nanny
said no more. I was safe. So we kept on getting chocolate until
one day the concierge told us, "My sister lost her job. I have no
more chocolate." I was stunned. I think that even today I still
miss the secrecy and the private joy of eating those chocolate
bars.

At home in the schoolroom, we got points rather than grades,
and at the end of each week we counted how many points we
had accumulated; each point represented a certain amount of
cents. Our earnings generally came to a figure of between five
and ten francs a week. It was fun counting the points and I
looked forward to the end of each week. "Mademoiselle," our
teacher, accepted our counting, and I cannot remember ever
having cheated. She took our points to the secretary and a day
or two later we received the money. It was an established fact
that Nanny would keep it for us. As years went by we accumulated a few hundred francs. Even though we never saw that
money—and didn't need it, as what would *we* need money
for?—we had a feeling of possession.

One summer at the seashore—I may have been thirteen—my
brother had two friends, one of whom kept trying to play with
me. There were rows of cabins right on the beach in which
people changed. With my brother, his friends, Maurice and
Roger, and my sister, we played hide-and-seek around the cabins.

One day it was quiet. Roger stood on a cliff next to me and said nothing. "Let's play," I offered.

"Yes, but what shall we do?" he asked.

"I don't know; what do you think?"

"I don't know either; what do you think?"

Neither of us had any suggestions. As he became more restless my discomfort grew. I was afraid he would run away. I, barely entering adolescence, started to search for something to say, but the awkward silence between us persisted. Suddenly Roger looked down the cliff and asked, "Do you think I could jump down?"

"Oh, no," I answered in a hurry, happy he had spoken and to be saved from such an uncomfortable situation.

"So you don't think I can jump?" I glanced down. The hill was not really high, but I had to keep up the conversation.

"No, of course you can't."

"Do you dare me?" he asked.

"Yes, I dare you," I said to make him happy. He smiled with satisfaction.

"Will you bet me that I can't?" Now the jump seemed unimportant; I was just happy to please him.

"Yes, I will bet you. Yes, yes." He waited for a moment and, as if to evaluate the distance below, looked down.

"What will you give me if I jump?"

"Ten francs!" I ventured, looking at him for approval. The moment he heard my offer he jumped with ease. I was ready to give him a warm "Bravo!" when he shouted, "You owe me ten francs," and ran away. I remained stunned as I looked down from so little height. It was no jump at all. What had I said? What had I done? Now I jumped and came back up. There was no one there. I went back to the cabin and said to my sister, "You see that cliff? I jumped down."

"So what?" she asked. And I said no more.

"Ten francs," I kept repeating to myself. "I owe ten francs." We did get a weekly allowance but Nanny "held" it and we never saw the money. What to do? Of course I could not ask Nanny for money. Though it was mine I would have felt as if I were asking Nanny for her own money. Anyhow, I knew she would say I didn't need it and I was too frightened to mention the bet.

Once again the fear of Nanny pushed me into secrecy. Any action outside her domination was forbidden; each taboo was enforced by a threat; danger loomed, danger was everywhere. I was becoming desperate so I finally told my sister and we started to search together for a solution. "Ask Father," Bethsabée suggested.

"How can I?" I asked.

"I don't know! But there's no other way."

I worried most of the night and the following morning as I greeted my parents before going out. I went as usual first to my mother, then to my father's room. He was in bed. I fussed around for a while. I knew I couldn't remain long in his room; I had to speak now.

"Father, if I ask you something, will you not tell anyone?"

"No, I won't."

"You are sure? You absolutely promise?"

"I promise." He seemed amused, but I was still in doubt.

"You won't even tell Mother?" I continued.

"No, my *cocotte*, of course not. What is it?" My sense of shame and guilt for offering money increased my fear, but my father was warm and kind, so I blurted out, "Can you give me ten francs?"

"Of course, sweetie," he said and handed me a ten-franc bill.

"Oh, thank you," I said, clutching it, "you won't tell?"

"No," he said with a smile. He didn't ask any questions and I didn't explain.

Now I had the money, but how could I give it to Roger without being seen? What if he were not on the beach? I managed to get the money down to the beach and as I waited for him I hid it in the cabin under the bench cover. When I finally saw him, I ran to him and said, "I have the ten francs I owe you." He smiled at me; I am sure he wondered why I didn't hand them over.

"I hid the money in the cabin. You must go and get it." I couldn't explain why I was using such a roundabout way and I was embarrassed. He looked at me with a strange expression.

"Why did you do that?" he asked.

"I didn't know when you would come—just go and get it when nobody is in the cabin." Because of my unusual behavior Roger started to think something was wrong.

"I was only joking," he said, after a slight hesitation.

As if he were ready to play, he came close to me and said, "I don't want your money." Suddenly I was panic-stricken. The ten francs couldn't remain in the cabin. Nanny would find them, and what would I say? I was all at once faced with an unexpected danger—the terrifying fact that I would be caught red-handed.

"No," I said, pushing him away, "go and get the money— you *have* to get it. It can't stay there. Get it . . . get it . . ."

"Okay, okay, if that's what you want."

"Yes, yes, you have to get it. It's under the seat cover, only don't let anyone see you."

When I knew that he had the money I felt an enormous relief. I had paid my debt and I was out of danger.

My next fear was of a different nature.

We never entered the elevator alone; Nanny forbade it. She called it the "lift." Years went by and danger loomed over our heads. Still with us, Nanny protected us against an imaginary danger, a danger she'd created. "Don't move, and don't talk, or you will stop the lift," she threatened. And we were quiet and silent, surrounded by a mysterious fear of some unknown danger. We accepted the fear, asked no questions, did not think.

I was already sixteen when I entered the house alone for the first time. Tired, I gazed at the stairs, four flights up, then at the empty elevator. It is ridiculous, I whispered to myself. Take the elevator—no one will know! I had been freed from Nanny for a year but fear remained. Of course, I had learned to live with fear since I saw danger everywhere. Cats in the dark corridors, footmen, butlers, men with white gloves coming from unknown quarters, a pantry I had never entered, bedrooms! Places I had never seen, places whose location I didn't know— the kitchen, for example. I wasn't even sure some of these places really existed. Yet I saw a closed door and men and women entering. Beyond a magic barrier lay an unknown world the domestics held. Was it a world of slavery, or a world of freedom? A world of pleasures, a world of dangers? I was excluded from whatever lay behind that mysterious world. I was an outsider.

Now I stood still in front of the elevator, hesitating. I had gone up in this very elevator for many years with Nanny, and later with Marcelle. My heart pounded as I entered, closed the door and read the floor number 4 over again before pressing it. Then I was off alone, on my way up, and suddenly I felt relieved. "It was so simple," I murmured. I could now see the last gate, my gate. I was almost up to it! I was happy, proud, relieved, but a little impatient. Just as I put my hand on the inside door, ready to pull, the elevator stopped. I was stunned, and didn't realize that I had stopped it myself by handling the door too soon. The little elevator in which I stood covered only the lower portion of the outside door, my door to freedom, leaving only a few feet of emptiness with a drop of four flights. I could climb—I had to get out. "What if I'm found?" I wondered. I didn't reason. Thinking was wiped out by panic. I stretched but couldn't reach the top of the outside gate. Then I jumped with all my power, but I hadn't noticed an iron bar above. My head hit that bar with such force that it broke off and came crashing to the floor beside me as I sat dazed and limp with fear. I didn't move for a while. I felt like a criminal caught in action, with no one to call, nowhere to turn. Shaking inside and not really knowing what I was doing, I pressed the button again and the elevator started up and covered the last few feet. I was safe! My adventure was over, already in the past. I got up and walked out. No one would ever need to know! But fear was still in me.

My mother also harbored fears. She overprotected my brother because she was afraid that if he walked to school alone a woman might pick him up!

It seems that what one fears most attracts the danger. Once in a while a hairdresser came right into the nursery to cut our hair. As he was using scissors on the back of my neck, I showed pleasure from the tickling sensation. He wasted no time. "Here is where it tickles," he said and took my hand to the swelling in his pants. I drew back in fear.

I had a very frightening experience when I was about fourteen years old. One day without any warning, Nanny said, "Go in the bedroom—there is someone who wants . . ." She didn't finish. I questioned with a stare. She urged me to the door, turning herself in the opposite direction. Filled with curiosity

and a sense of pride, I went to the door. A visitor for me, breaking the monotony of our routine! I was cheerful. Who could it
be? I entered. Two men were settled with some kind of machin-
ery. I stood waiting awkwardly.

"I want to look at your throat," said one of the doctors as he
held a white cloth. Silently I came closer and lifted my arms.
"No," he nodded, indicating with a sign that the sheet was to
go above my shoulders. I remained very still as he started
wrapping it around my whole body once, twice, three times,
and fear mounted in me each time it went around. I stood now
straight and mummified, helplessly at the mercy of the two
strangers. One of them sat and held me between his knees
while the other covered my face with a mask attached to the
machine. The ether smelled dangerous as it became hard to
breathe. I couldn't move; in spite of the desperation of my position, my mind started searching for some miraculous defense.
Slowly, almost imperceptibly, I turned my head, twisting my
mouth toward fresh air, but I gained no ground. The doctor's
knees tightened, two hands gripped my head and the suffocat-
ing mask closed in. For a few seconds I held my breath—a dark
swirl—nothing.

A few weeks after the operation I was still weak with fear. I
slowed down before turning corners, my throat was still burning, and that awful smell of ether—it was everywhere. I looked
at a closed door on my right, wondering what hid behind it,
then I entered a corridor, long and dark. On one side huge furniture stood against the wall. The black ebony with its ivory
incrustations cast the shadows of many past centuries. I stood
at one end. It seemed that ether was still around me. Well, I
thought, why don't you run? The cat hides behind those ward-
robes and springs. Why don't you run? I looked down, brought
my arms close to my body. I seemed to shrivel up, as if I could
make myself still smaller, then walked step by step, very
slowly. I stopped in front of the *Salon des Chasseurs*, the Hunters' Room where the male company gathered before the hunting parties. I opened the door, glanced around. The room
seemed unused, cold, forbidding, a little frightening, with deer
heads and their huge antlers on the walls and the stuffed
pheasants seemingly alive but dead. It was part of the men's
world where I did not belong. I retreated and continued my
expedition down the heavy channels of the castle.

Yes, fear was the story of my life.

[13]

Socializing

Because we grew up so sheltered, the inward thrust of my feelings slowed my development and hindered me for many years. At eight years old I was still taught at home by a private teacher. Because Colette was my only friend, I did not learn how to deal with a group of children and, probably because I had a sister, it was easier to relate on a one-to-one basis. My social life remained damaged. As an adult, my inability to communicate prompted people to think of me as cold and snobbish.

This difficulty in taking my place among friends showed up first when my mother, realizing we were too isolated, decided to invite our cousins. When I was twelve she arranged a small party with my friend Colette, her brother Gilbert, and four Rothschild cousins.

We were excited when we realized our guests were coming but, not knowing what to expect, I dared not rejoice. Prudence had become part of me. I was also becoming expert in withholding, so the little excitement that accompanies new expectations quickly turned to apprehension.

Though we were always clean, we were somewhat more dressed up than usual. A large tea was prepared with an assortment of cakes. Finally the cousins arrived.

For a few moments we all stared with embarrassment, but soon the power of youth took over. Movement and noise filled the austerity of the castle. My brother shared in the laughing and talking. I trailed after the group silently, watching and trying to understand. The girls, screaming and giggling, were bending over and the boys were pinching their behinds. "Mine is bigger," shouted Colette, "try again." Others shouted, "No, mine is bigger." "Try me"—"Now me," and the boys went from one girl to the other over and over again, each time with new excitement. I moved among them silently, but I was left out. I came closer, trying to make myself noticed. As nothing helped, I bent over. "Try me," I ventured shyly. No one saw me. Suddenly I became angry and yelled, "Try me," shoving my rear end right at one of the boys. Success! He stopped for a second. "You!" he said with some surprise. My heart started to pound and I tried sticking out even more. But he barely touched me. "You're tiny," he shouted, running off and leaving me stranded in my awkwardly bent position. "You touched only half," I muttered. "It was only half," but no one heard me. Misjudged, humiliated, and confused, I could not explain; I could not impose myself. So I walked among my "friends" quietly, trying not to seem conspicuous.

I continued to meet my cousins and other children on our daily walks in the Champs Élysées or in the Bois-de-Boulogne, but I have very little recollection of those children as my relationship to them was too superficial to break through Nanny's oppressive fortress. Colette remained my only real friend. We were the same age and had the same social standing, which was not the case when we played in Ferrières with the caretaker's children, Betty and James Hunter.

Mostly I lived among servants, men and women I saw every day but knew only their first names. They were there to serve and I never wondered about their private lives. I took for granted their apparent absence of human reactions. My father screamed at them because he was quick-tempered, but he was not mean; they knew it and didn't hold his temper against him. On the other hand, my mother always spoke very politely but with an undertone of superiority, which could hurt or humiliate. That embarrassed and awoke resentment in me.

A polite exchange was the extent of my relationship to the anonymous community of all the servants. Of course, this condition was common in those times; familiarity with the domestics didn't exist. But my "social relations" with the help were curbed by Nanny's jealous and possessive nature. Once, when my mother's maid Juliette passed us in the hall, Bethsabée, who was two years old, greeted her with open arms, calling, "Yulie, Yulie." Nanny very angrily screamed at her to stop and never do that again, and my sister never spoke to Juliette again.

This absence of relationship with the help continued until one day when I was fourteen and a new maid, engaged to work for Nanny, entered the nursery. She was called Marie, but there were other Maries, so her name was changed to Renée— Renée Ovise. She was thin, frail, and very quiet, with short, flat hair drawn back. She could have been a model for one of Kathe Kollwitz's drawings (this famous painter depicted mostly the poor and underprivileged). Renée moved silently as a fleeting shadow of misery. She spoke seldom and very softly, but kindness emanated from her. When Nanny shouted at me unfairly, I glanced at Renée and her sad eyes, deeply sunk into her bony cheeks, told me she understood. I had a friend.

Occasionally I tried a question, to which Renée's answer in a low, toneless voice was "Yes" or "No" or just a nod and a mumbling sound with a kind smile. Though we didn't speak to each other, there was a real exchange between us. She felt for me, and I think she knew even then that I liked her. We stayed on the same side of the fence for many years.

And even though she was one of the servants, Renée became my best friend after Colette. Maybe that accounts for the good relations I have today with the people who work for me, such as Mayme Bell who has worked for me in the house for thirty-eight years; when she is gone on vacation for a month I miss the friend, not her work.

[14]

Sports

I was athletically gifted and loved all exercise: the swinging bar, the rings, bicycling. Riding was my first sport, a noncompetitive activity. We rode only for enjoyment, and I really did enjoy it. Riding seemed to be inherent to the Rothschild family. Every member rode except for my mother, who was afraid of horses and would never attempt riding. The pride of horses showed in the races, and in England, in the cruel sport of deer hunting. My paternal grandmother, whom I never knew, rode almost until the day of her death, and I admired my brother Guy for riding the racehorses on the training field.

We were taught to ride, but I never brushed a horse, saddled, or unsaddled one. I never tightened the strap under a horse's belly, never handled the bridle or the bit. I not only never got a horse out of his stall, but I don't remember ever even seeing our horses' stalls. And we always rode very quiet horses, with our teacher, never with friends or family.

Tuesdays and Fridays I changed into riding clothes. Riding was such a welcome activity. As my sister and I rode the old-fashioned sidesaddle with two prongs for the legs to hang onto I wore high leather boots, a very elegant gabardine suit with a skirt, and to protect our heads, if we fell, we also wore a hard black hat called a melon hat.

Mr. Bernard, an old experienced man who called himself a teacher, waited for us with three very calm horses. To get us up on our mounts he made a step with his hands, interlocking his fingers, and shoved us up. We never considered trying to climb by ourselves. Mr. Bernard always accompanied us on our one-hour promenade. One day something frightened the horses, and my sister and I broke off into a nice little gallop. Although we couldn't stop the horses or direct them, *we* weren't particularly frightened.

But Mr. Bernard became frantic. He galloped behind us screaming, and this, of course, only stirred the horses into more speed. They laid back their ears and gripped the bit. When we reached the end of the field they jumped the ditch. I was having fun, an adventure, but poor Mr. Bernard was in a panic. Finally he used his head. He took a short-cut and, coming in front of us, stopped our horses with ease. Though nothing had really happened, I think I was pleased to be back in control, and I felt a little sorry for Mr. Bernard.

I looked forward to riding. When I rode, all the muscles in my body became alive. I loved the wind in my face, when trotting or cantering. We went under huge chestnut trees, then out in the fields. The horse, continually chewing on his bit, kept in close contact with me. His body was warm and I blended in with his movements. It was satisfying to feel master of the situation. Though once in a while a rabbit or a rock would cause my horse to shy, I seldom fell off.

One day as I was bicycling around the park in Ferrières, the caretaker's daughter Betty Hunter pointed ahead. "You see that corner. Last week my horse stepped in a hole and we both fell."

"Who were you with?" I asked.

"I was alone, of course, and I had a hard time catching him."

"Alone! You don't mean you ride alone?"

"Well, of course! Why not?"

"If you get hurt . . . if something . . . if . . ." I was stuttering. But what was so terrible? Was Betty abandoned to reckless dangers? She was an employee's daughter. She rode alone, in dungarees, with maybe only a sweater. Her head! I looked at her long blond hair as fear, pity, and envy kept me silent. Not even a hat, no protection, nothing on her head! Was she that neglected? She looked back at me with some irony.

"Who do you think would have time to ride with me?!" Her

parents worked for my father. Of course there could be no paid man to serve her, to protect her, to boss her! Yes, I was in a different class! I always rode clean, shiny horses with immaculate saddle and reins. The pride of wearing high shiny boots, fitted pants, a voluminous shirt seemed to be part of the joy of riding. I felt as if I were conquering the world. Of course I was so protected that I was never really exposed to danger. My sense of adventure was limited to circling the well-known alleys. I looked again at the faraway corner where Betty and her horse had fallen in a mole hole, the rugged little clearing by the woods. Poor Betty, I thought, and part of me felt superior. She was my friend, we were alike—and yet, I couldn't tell. Beneath my entangled feelings hid a little sadness and envy. As I felt superior I caught myself looking up to Betty. She wasn't afraid to venture out alone with a horse who was not well cleaned and, maybe, not so calm! She went alone on any field, explored any corner of the dark, mysterious woods. How wonderful that must feel! But I could never dare, even in thoughts, to go down to the life of a proletariat and up to freedom, adventure, danger, real living! "How did you get back on the horse?"

"Oh, I found a stump, climbed on, it was easy."

I said no more, but I knew that even a stump would not help me with such a voluminous skirt and the two prongs and no one to hold my horse.

One day, bicycling around the golf course with Betty, I got a sudden urge to play golf (I had not yet learned).

"Do you play golf?" I asked.

"No."

"Nor do I."

But soon after, I was given a set of clubs and told that I was going to learn to play golf. I went back to the little English house, but this time in the car. A very young man, Jean Alzuguren, and a little boy, a caddy, were waiting for me. Jean took the bag of clubs. He set a basket of balls in front of me on the lawn. My young teacher showed me how to hold the stick and how to hit a ball far away. When the balls were all scattered away the little boy went out and picked them up and I started all over again. Soon I hit the balls clean and far. Then we started walking around the golf course. There were nine holes, hard to discern and yet only a few minutes from the castle. I always seemed to get on the green or close to it in one, two, or three strokes, but then I fumbled around before I got the ball in the hole, and that made me angry. I played several times a week. Jean was always there. I never knew where he came from or where he lived. Though I wasn't told, I sensed that he was there to serve me. But he was young and he took pleasure in my progress. I looked forward to those games. My sense of perfection drove me to stand for hours and hit balls further and more consistently. Always there, Jean stood by me before each stroke. As I gripped the club, his eyes concentrated on my hands, following the upswing of my arms; and with the support of his look, I hit hard. "That is beautiful," he murmured. I smiled and he returned my smile. His penetrating glance seemed to go through me, injecting vitality and a burning desire to play well. But what was "well"? I wondered. Jean was a young professional. Bogey or par set a standard. Soon I was comparing my score to par, getting very moody when I missed a shot and much too self-contented when I made a good one. Jean kept complimenting me.

Years went by. I still played with Jean and often stood in one place and practiced hitting "drives." I liked Jean's attention. We never spoke personally, but tension was growing between us. At times I responded to his restlessness. Then I asked him to teach me a few words in his language, Basque, as his family came from the south of Bordeaux. I started speaking to him, throwing in a few Basque words, and I could feel tension.

"What is the matter?" I asked. He glanced at me and said, "Nothing." Once he said, "You know," but I insisted, "No, I don't! What's the matter? What's the matter?" I kept pushing and he retreated.

"Nothing is the matter—just play." I was never sure if he really had any feelings for me, but I thought he did.

When I first started playing golf I enjoyed the challenge, the need to become good. For a few years I played alone, competing only against perfection. I was deeply involved in trying to reach par. The cruel competitive aspect of winning and losing had not become an issue until I was entered in a tournament, and was completely unprepared—technically, emotionally, and mentally—for the event.

Unexpectedly I was taken to a golf club and entered in a tournament. Bewildered by such an experience, I floundered. The clubhouse was very attractive. Having practically never been in a public place, I was scared. Just walking through the main hall made me feel awkward and very uneasy. My legs shook as I stood in front of my ball on the first tee. A woman whom I didn't know was going to go around with me. A caddy whom I didn't know was carrying my clubs. Although I didn't know how far the first green was I lifted my arms and hit, but the ball didn't fly through the air with a clean whipping sound as at home. I tore out a lump of grass and the ball went bumping to the right only a short distance. I was stunned. Then I hit it again and again and it took six or seven strokes to reach the green. I felt as if I had never played before. Golf had become a new game for me and I wasn't up to it. It never entered my head that I was reduced by stage fright. No, I just knew that I wasn't up to the rest of the world. I was an outcast. My opponent seemed to belong to a level far beyond me. I forgot that I really could do better. I was in a competition but I was trailing far behind. I was not even really competing. I knew that I could never enter their world.

As we approached the ninth hole, I felt relief. But to my utter surprise, there were eighteen holes! I had never played eighteen holes. As I kept on walking I got more and more tired. I was ashamed, angry, and crushed at the same time.

Days later when I saw Jean he asked, "What happened?"

I said only, "I played badly."

"It doesn't matter, you'll do better next time." I looked at him and felt warmth. I started hitting balls. They flew straight and far. "Like a champ," he said.

"The other day I couldn't hit at all," I told him. "I just don't know why." Now I could play and I was pleased, but that didn't make up for my previous ridiculous performance. Deep in me I did not believe I could compete but I knew I would try again.

It was nice to be with Jean. He liked me, he believed in me. Being with him felt good. But in spite of the unspoken feeling between us I knew he was paid to teach me, to play with me. I kept on practicing alone with Jean. "You're terrific," he would say. "You should win." So I entered tournaments from time to time but never came anywhere near winning.

One day my mother said to my father, "Did you hear about that seventeen-year-old girl Simone Thion de la Chaume, who won the National Championship? She also won in England and will go to America. She is absolutely terrific."

"Yes," answered my father, "she is amazing." After a short silence my mother added, casually, "It must be nice to have a daughter like that." She spoke almost to herself as I sat listening, but then looked toward me and said, "But of course you could never . . ."

No, I could never! I was crushed and angry, hammered down with a brick, ground into the earth, stamped forever as a failure, and yet with such a rage within me that I knew I would *never* stop trying. Did I want to prove my mother wrong when I believed she was right, or was I dreaming of making her proud of me—reaching the impossible? Perhaps I simply hoped to live up to what she wanted. (Years later, Simone Thion de la Chaume married the tennis champion René La Coste and we all became good friends.)

As my mother took singing and golf lessons, she probably had hidden dreams of her own achievements. She never improved and may have projected her own limitations on me, although she certainly was not aware that she was destroying me.

We spent summers in Saint-Jean-de-Luz, a small beach resort near Arcachon in the south of France where there was a very nice golf course. So I kept on playing. I kept entering tournaments. I had to win. My original defeat was still alive in me. I had improved my game, competing had become a burning force, and I played well enough: yes, I *had* to win. I started well, I was on top, but when it dawned on me that I was going to win my insides scrambled up in fear and I fell apart. I was in despair and in a rage. "I threw it! I can't do it! I can't . . . I can't . . ." and I kept trying, repeating the same pattern of failure. I felt incapable, like a beaten dog. My mother had said, "It would be nice to have a daughter like that . . . but of course you could never . . ." No, I would never be good. I would always be an outcast. I was still a loser.

[15]

Authority

Nanny was the authority. She had full power over us but to her that was insufficient because my parents held the real authority. They had hired her and they could dismiss her. We knew it (or did we?), but we didn't feel it. As my mother left after her goodnight kiss, Nanny would grumble and say, "Your mother has no manners. She is rude to me." Her reproachful tone implied it was my fault. So when my parents left the nursery we asked fearfully, "Were they nice to you?"

Once every few months, when Nanny had a day off, I rose to authority. My mother took us to a park where children of all ages played on swings, ran with balls, jumped and screamed. When insecurity replaced oppression I took over. My sister asked, "May I go over there?"

"Yes," my mother said, but my sister still looked at me and waited.

"It's all right, you may go," my mother repeated. But Beth-sabée would only move when *I* approved. Nanny's little darling, who was good when I wasn't, who got all the favors, whose importance belittled me, now appeared to shrink into her real position of my baby sister, while I grew proud of my new power. I had become Nanny. I was the authority. I felt satisfaction in protecting my sister but also pleasure in having her at my mercy.

As my motherly feelings awoke, my day in the park became marred. I walked over to a very sweet baby of about fourteen months. She greeted me with a big smile and pointed to the swings. I lifted her and started pushing the seat of her swing. She laughed and I was happy, but I was only ten years old and didn't have very good judgment. I got carried away and pushed the swing a little too hard. She slid off to the ground, and the descending seat hit her on the head. Although she screamed, luckily she wasn't hurt. My fright and despair were more damaging to me than her bump on the head was to her.

I now realize that my mother couldn't assert her authority because she spent too little time with us; she never stayed long enough with us to get annoyed and angry. Love is less penetrating if there is never anger. If with one's mother one can never scream and slam the door, a distance is created, and as a result, respect replaces closeness. But my mother *did* love us and we never doubted it; and she *was* head of the household. Butler, footmen, and maids jumped to serve her. The cook came to her room every morning to plan the next day's menus and discuss the previous day's meals, and when my mother sat with her secretary she was not to be disturbed.

And my father depended on her to organize his social life— dinner parties, dances, hunting parties, and she was ready to sacrifice anything to please him.

Then one day I found myself in an authoritative position and not able to live up to it. That day from the bedroom I gazed at the ducks peacefully gliding on a quiet lake beyond which the park extended to the infinite. I loved to bicycle through the mysterious meanders of this unpredictable park on moss-covered alleys darkened by thick foliage of chestnut trees. This was Ferrières, rich with myriads of hidden lives. I never knew exactly where I would come out; sometimes I would land in the *faisanderie* for a while and watch the little gray monkeys with black circles around their eyes, which made them appear inquisitive. At other times I would look for the bleeding chest of the *colombes poignardées* or ride around the golf course with its well-groomed greens. But this day I turned to the main alley which continued deep into the woods. I passed apprehensively between the two bronze statues of hounds assaulting a wild boar, then, on both sides of the alley, huge white and mauve balls of rhododendrons. The mild dampness added to the mysterious nostalgia of the century-old trees. A baby rabbit rustled dead leaves and I pedaled faster as time seemed to stand still. Now I entered a farm and was somewhat relieved to find life, to smell manure, and to see a flock of geese. The farmer's children were around, but I couldn't play with them. Frozen, they looked at me from a distance as if I were some unusual species. But even that was better than being alone. Today their mother surprised me when she asked if I would come in and talk to them. I could hardly believe my luck, and my heart was pounding as I entered a very modest room with a musty smell. Would I know what to say? Would the children play with me?

"Please sit down." She was hovering over me. Embarrassed, I obeyed. Then a sudden outburst from her: "Please speak to your father for us, we did nothing wrong! We have seven children! It is terrible! Help us! What will we do? Help us, please, please."

I was bewildered, not knowing what she was talking about and afraid to question. My silence seemed to make me the hard accomplice to a powerful father. Embarrassment, shame, pity froze as I heard myself saying, "Yes, I will speak to him, I will do what I can."

"Thank you, please help us, please, please . . ." Cornered by this begging appeal, I awkwardly edged my way back to my bicycle. Though I felt I was completely helpless, I was an authority in the farmer's eyes.

With a new load, I started back, but slowed down as I came closer to home. I even took detours, circling by the lake. I finally crossed the brick bridge and entered the castle without stopping to feed the deer. I didn't follow my desire to rush to my father but, nursing my secret mission, slowly climbed first the back stairs, then the majestic marble ones. As I mounted, my eyes fixed on the red carpet. I stopped where the stairs divided into two equal ascents, both leading to the square corridor, and eventually to my room. I glanced at the dark marble rail and felt an urge to caress the amethyst grapes at its base, as if touching a stone would help turn my mixed emotions into concrete thoughts.

Several hours went by before I went down for dinner. When I entered the hall my mother and father were both sitting by the fire. My father wore a smoking jacket as usual and my mother, living up to the formality of their intimacy, had changed into a green velvet dress.

"You're late," my mother said, glancing at her watch. It was not much past a quarter to eight. I stood by the marble plaque over the fireplace and read the inscription written in old French:

Douce est la vie à la bien suivre
Emmy soyet printemps soyet hyvers
Sous blanche neige ou rameaux verts
Quand vrays amis nous la font vivre
Ains leur place à touts est ici
Comme aux vieux aux jeunes aussi

Life is gentle if followed right
Whether spring or whether winter
Under white snow or green boughs
When you share it with true friends
This home is open to all
The old and young as well

As I was looking for words, the black, shiny busts with their colorful turbans and precious earrings kept smiling on each side of the chimney. I was just about to speak when both sides of a heavy door opened and a butler in black livery announced with a slight bow, *"Madame la Baronne est servi."* And the three of us marched by the inlaid Italian cabinets, crossed a large hallway and entered the dining room. Dinner was quiet. Very little was said. I was searching for a way to approach my father. After dinner we went back into the immense hall for coffee. My mind was still on the farm.

"I went to Pont-Carré," I started. "The farmers spoke to me." My mother glanced at me but didn't pay attention to what I was saying. Looking at my father, I continued: "They asked me to speak to you." I was suddenly interrupted by an angry flow.

"How dare they! They must get out! Leave me alone . . ."
Heavy silence enveloped my father's anger as my mother

stared into the peaceful flames in the fireplace. Afraid of his anger, I shivered; but I had promised to help the farmers. Gathering courage, I continued, "They have seven children." This infuriated my father even more but now, aware of being the last hope of a large family, I insisted. *"What* did they do? Why must they go?" Pushed, my father started yelling with an incomprehensible outpouring of sounds, working himself into a rage. Embarrassed, scared, and full of hate, I fought tears.

As I've said my father was quick-tempered and when angry he couldn't control himself, but his outbursts never lasted. He stopped as abruptly as he had started. The storm was over. Lifting his hand as if he were going to pat my hair, he smiled. *"Ma cocotte . . ."* Without moving, I withdrew abruptly. He got up and walked toward the billiard table, his smile slowly fading.

(Unfortunately, it was much later that I understood that my father didn't like having to fire the farmers. Due to his inherent difficulty in explaining his views, anger usually covered his confused and contradictory feelings.) From the huge old Italian cabinets inlaid with mother-of-pearl he opened a drawer and found three ivory balls. The red one had become light pink with age. The two white ones with their soft veins had mellowed into a silky weight. He reached for the cue and, rubbing its top with blue chalk, started playing for his daily exercise. Usually I played with him. It was fun trying to hit the balls. I loved the worn, faded green cloth punctured in spots with tiny holes where someone had accidentally hit the table instead of the ball. I enjoyed the precision it took to play and I loved competing with my father. When the ball didn't quite reach its goal, both father and daughter twisted their bodies, as if such contortions could change its direction. Each carambole was recorded. We both loved our genetic intimacy and didn't need conversation; I had always enjoyed and looked forward to playing with him. But this evening I stayed by the fireplace and let him play alone.

[16]

School

Our governess's only function was to teach us. So after breakfast we went to the room next to our bedroom, the schoolroom, and Mademoiselle dwelled on spelling, grammar, arithmetic, history, geography.

Although it was nice to be away from Nanny, the hours often passed slowly, and because we were taught alone at home without the stimulation of other children, we had no incentive. If we didn't learn, no one cared. As there was nothing at stake, we put no concentration or effort into our studies. Mademoiselle tried to win our favor, so if anything happened to be right she would be most encouraging. "That is good, very good," she told us, and we were pleased. We learned how to enjoy undeserved praise. Nothing happened if I didn't read an assignment.

Nanny, of course, didn't like Mademoiselle, who was a threat to her supremacy, so we never saw Mademoiselle outside of the schoolroom. Several years later when our routine became familiar to us, I was told one day, "Next week you will start going to school twice a week." I was sent to a private school called Le Cours Bouté de Monvel, after the dwarfed and crippled old woman who owned and ran it. Her students quickly overlooked her deformity because she was capable and alert, and she made her classes very alive.

Around other children I was totally bewildered. Mademoiselle remained in the classroom. She sat without interfering in one of the chairs against the wall. In a fog, I spoke to no one. I never knew the answer to questions asked. Even worse, most of the time I didn't know what the teacher was talking about.

When the teacher left the room at the end of each class, all the other children rushed onto her platform, crowding around her desk. In a daze, at first I didn't pay attention, but one day I started to wonder what they were doing. As time went by, I became more and more curious. Finally I decided to find out, so I followed the others to the teacher's desk. I was part of the scramble, though I didn't know what to look for.

"Don't push," said a stranger. Then, looking at me, "What do *you* want?"

"I want to see."

"You!" she laughed. "There is nothing for *you* to see. *You* probably have a zero." She treated me as a failure, and I felt ridiculous. Of course I knew that I wasn't up with the class, but what did that have to do with a zero? I was not familiar with grades and she didn't explain. "What do you mean?" I ventured.

"Maybe you think you have a six!" she sneered. (That was the highest grade, although I didn't know it.) She turned and giggled with other girls, pointing to me. The top girl in the class, Louise Burin des Rosiers, was pretty and nice, so I turned to her.

"What did you see?" I asked, not quite revealing that I didn't know what they were looking at.

"Oh, I have a six, which gives me a five-and-a-half average for the week."

"How do you know?"

"I just looked."

"Are all the grades up there?"

"Of course—you didn't know?"

"No," I admitted. "Mine too?"

"Yes, every grade is in her ledger. She leaves it on the desk—go and look."

One day during a class the teacher went over the standing of every student. She started with the best, gradually working her way down to the weaker ones. I sat and waited with a heavy heart. Finally she paused. My name had not come up.

"And now I have to mention the three girls who are too far behind to be called even the tail of the class. One is Odile Kamerere," and everyone turned to look at a round, red-faced jovial girl whose hair was cut short like a boy, but curly, which made her head look like a fluffy ball. Her eyes were sparkling; she appeared to be so alert I was surprised to be in a group with her. "Odile," continued the teacher, "has an excuse. She is a violinist and, I understand, a very good one. She is part of the Conservatoire de Musique de Paris and she practices the violin six hours a day. But the other two—" she lifted her hands as if to let them express the hopelessness of the situation—"Jeanine made only half a point this week, and you—" she turned her crippled little deformed body and looked straight at me—"and you are the very last."

After the class, Mademoiselle went up to her and I overheard, "She is too far behind; she cannot follow."

That evening I kept thinking of Odile Kamerere. "She's lucky," I told myself, she is so lucky—so very lucky—she is a violinist, a good one; that is so much more than making good grades in school.

My parents were told that I was not up to the class and my father patted me, with tenderness in his eyes. "She is a girl. It doesn't matter. *Ma pauvre cocotte!* She will get married. Girls don't have to learn."

Except for the English class, where he was expected to be first as we spoke English before we knew any French, my brother was only an average student. Once he came home and during lunch, while the butler in white gloves announced, before pouring, "Château Lafite, 1900," my father asked my brother, "How did it go?"

"I was only second this week. There is another boy—"

But my father didn't let him finish. He started yelling, "Second, it is a disgrace! With your background it should be easy." He didn't look at my brother when he got angry, but seemed to eat faster. Words were intermingled with grumbling sounds. "You are lazy," he continued, "a lazy good-for-nothing. Second! I don't want to hear that—" He hesitated as everyone was silent. My mother tried to hide her embarrassment with a constricted, casual smile. The butler kept going around the table, serving lobster *à l'armoricaine*, tender tails swimming in a lus-

cious red sauce. My father threw a furtive glance at my
mother, maybe because he needed support and encouragement, but her eyes were fixed on an empty plate.

My brother tried to profit from this instant of weakness when
my father hesitated. Pointing at me, he said, "Why don't you
ever say anything to *her*? You pick on me!"

That was just what my father needed. "Because she is a
girl." His voice was loud, and the seriousness of his look im-
posed fear. "Second!" he repeated with disgust, "I will not
hear that *ever* again. You understand?"

That evening I lay in bed with bottled-up feelings. "Boys
have to work! Why, I wondered—why don't *I* have to? I am
incapable in school but I am good in my father's eyes. Why?
Oh yes, I remember, I am a girl." Yet in school there were a lot
of girls, all of them capable except Odile. But she had an excuse—she was a violinist—a good one. I got up and went to the
window. The Place de la Concorde seemed spacious, illumi-
nated at night. Further to the left, I saw the Tuileries. They told
me in the schoolroom that Marie Antoinette's head had been
cut off just over there. I pressed my finger against the window
and shivered. "Get back to bed," murmured my sister, "she is
coming!"

We had solfège lessons, which I liked. But I wondered: "If I
don't need to learn, why the lessons? Yes, of course, I need to
learn, but to my parents it doesn't matter if I don't." I hadn't
understood that they wanted me to learn the skills which were
important socially. At that time music was fashionable, even
for a girl. Confusing! The teacher played different melodies and
different rhythms. I stood next to her, singing, or, more accu-
rately, naming the notes and beating time with my right hand.
We also had dancing lessons once a week. I don't know—
maybe Bethsabée and I were slow in learning, but we never got
past elementary exercises. I felt awkward and stiff and usually
tired. But I could get out on the golf course and hit a ball farther than any woman in France.

I went back to bed, my father's voice still filling my heart
with fear. He screamed at the help in the middle of meals.
"The fish is not good," he would grumble, holding his plate at

arm's length, "take it away, it smells fishy," and a footman in blue uniform with gold buttons would rush to the rescue: *"Oui, Monsieur le Baron!"*

"Tell that cook, tell that idiot to come and see me after dinner."

Flashes of memory kept coming and going through my head. I saw a crippled dwarf pointing at me, saying, "You are the very last!"

I had asked Mademoiselle, "Will I have my head cut off?"

"Of course not. Marie Antoinette's head was cut off because King Louis XVI was bad to the people. There was unrest. And besides, *you* are not a queen."

"No, I am not a queen," I whispered, "but I live in a palace. My father fired the farmer with his seven children. He yells at the men who serve him."

As I tossed in bed, my sister asked, "Can't you sleep?" I didn't answer. Suddenly I felt a burning desire for love. My flesh was aching as I was alone in bed. "I have to do something," I murmured, "do something great."

"What did you say?" Bethsabée asked.

"Nothing. Leave me alone." Then suddenly I asked, "Do you think I could play the violin?"

"I suppose so, but what for?"

Later I asked my mother. "I don't know," she said. She seemed uncertain. "The violin is a difficult instrument."

"I could learn," I urged.

"You need a good pitch to play violin. But if you want to try . . ." I was given a violin and again private lessons, one a week. Every day I sat for an hour trying to practice, which meant scratching in the first position, mostly on the G string. I spent a large part of the hour daydreaming, and often I would sweep the furniture with my bow. Deep in me I wanted to play, but I didn't know how to practice. I was particularly bewildered when my teacher said, "Play the open strings. D is too low; don't you hear it?" Annoyed, she would grab the violin away from me and tune it. When she left I ran to the piano, hit a ré, closed my eyes, sang it, hit another note, but couldn't guess its name. I played the same note on the violin as on the piano and discovered that if I hit an A on the piano and held it with the pedal I could match it on the violin. With this system I could tune my instrument. But that was as far as it went. I had no natural ability for music. I made practically no progress, and the daily hour of practice seemed harder every time. I had asked for it, and what was I doing?

In the evening as I lay in bed, tears rolled down my cheeks silently, uncontrollably. When Miss Swainston came to check on us I curled up and made her believe I was asleep. Hours went by and the tears kept rolling down. "I wish my mother would be hiding behind that door, just once," I murmured.

Eventually the violin lessons were dropped, and, of course, I was not in school anymore, so I spent all my so-called learning hours alone at home in the schoolroom. Once the teacher gave me an assignment to write a story—anything I liked. When she corrected it she said, with astonishment, "I just can't understand. You write as if you had always lived alone on a deserted island."

[17]

Three Worlds

When I was between twelve and fourteen years old (I don't remember exactly), my routine changed. Instead of eating every meal in the nursery I began to have meals with my parents. Ever since my young years when Bethsabée wouldn't eat and I wasn't offered the dishes I liked, or when I had to bicycle deep into the park for a chocolate bar, food became important to me.

With my parents, meals took on a different meaning; they became a ritual. Every day before joining my parents for dinner I changed clothes and cleaned up, as in preparation for an important event. Yes, it was important to join my mother and father and to get away from the nursery; but lunches, though very good, were not simple. Menus consisted of a dish to start with, the main course with potatoes and vegetables, a salad, a dessert, cheese, then fruit. Often, sitting through six courses seemed long and cumbersome. Cooking in France was considered an art. It symbolized a high standard of living, refinement, and sometimes an opportunity to show off. But to me it seemed more like a primitive worship. I was annoyed by the endless analysis of the sauce, by the time spent on discussing the quality of the lamb—did it have a faint "woolly" taste? Did the fish taste fishy? To me, discussions which exaggerated the importance of food were an empty waste of time, and often embarrassing. But in spite of the endless detailed criticism of the food I enjoyed quality dishes such as a poached egg on a purée of partridge.

Before meals with my parents we gathered in the *Salon Vert*. Though I accepted its name, I never really noticed the green silk on the walls between the wood paneling, nor the thick green curtains. Nor did I much notice the numerous paintings. Of course, I saw the man in blue looking at a globe. Except for a streak of light coming from the window, the *Geographer* by Vermeer seemed dirty. Nor was I impressed by a painting of a magnificent group of people by Pieter de Hoogh. The man sitting at a table smoking a pipe was leaning back on the bench, his feet extended and crossed. Another man was pouring wine from a pitcher into a glass held out by a woman sitting at the table and a small dog was sleeping on the floor. However, I liked a small head by Van Ostade of a peasant woman dressed in red with a white bonnet around her head. Occasionally I looked at a Gerard Dou which had a man leaning out of a window, holding a violin and smiling. Rather than a smile, it seemed to me like a sardonic laugh. Rembrandt, Holbein, Rubens, and Van Moll were part of the collection. I often looked at a woman drinking water from a glass, a stemmed glass so fine, so real, and yet to me it was only a glass. Once again the name Ter Borch entered one ear and went out the other. It didn't register until many years later when the painting was declared a copy! Yes, in the *Salon Vert*, where we met before lunch, where we sat after meals while my father drank coffee and brandy, where my mother, in a deep armchair, sipped her afternoon tea among Sevres vases on inlaid tables and chests, I sat carefully on those brocaded sixteenth-century chairs.

Across a small hallway we entered the everyday dining room. As I sat eating, I saw Fragonard's man and lady on each side of the chimney and two full-size children by Goya on the opposite wall.

Coming down for meals, only one flight from the nursery, I entered a different world, my mother's and father's world. The nursery, my parents' world, and my inner dreams threw me into three totally different atmospheres; I battled three worlds. Nanny always found me bad; she often called me "a dirty

French girl." At best, I was only her beloved Bethsabée's older sister. Downstairs, I was treated like a princess. My parents loved me but didn't understand me. With them I was the oldest of the girls, but they considered Bethsabée more intelligent. The third world of sadness, anger, dreams of achievements extended deep within me.

Upstairs the maids kept the linen room door always open but we never entered, and that cast a mystery over a community from which we were excluded. Sex filled the air, hypocritically hidden and yet everywhere. Madame Edouard, the head maid, went down the corridor with a man at her side, his hand on her rear end. When they heard my footsteps they hastened around the corner and miraculously vanished.

Downstairs I was quiet and polite, a pretty doll, a puppet to be served and catered to. A shadow of myself, I seemed to become merely an object in the private museum.

In the schoolroom upstairs I sat with my teacher and books that I didn't read or study. I was considered lazy, ignorant, and dumb. I would have liked to learn, but didn't know how to study, so I retreated into my private world, a world of passion, a world of fantasy in which I was famous, a champion, a musician, or even a writer.

In my parents' world, I was told, "Girls do not need to study." A beautiful necklace, a pretty dress, clean hands and face, a lovely smile—what could make a woman more admired! Day by day the walls thickened between me and the outside world. As I got locked in more deeply, my dreams became more intense and less clear. I moved among people as an unnoticed shadow, neither good nor bad, a living shell. Within that shell a boiling tornado would drive me toward great achievements. Which achievements? That didn't matter anymore. As a blistering sun burns through dense fog, I would shine in a luminous world of my own. Whatever I did I knew was good. Opinions upstairs, downstairs didn't exist. I was famous because I deserved to be and the people around me didn't even deserve to know. So among nurses, teachers, maids, butlers, footmen, a mother, a father, cooks, gardeners, concierges, Rembrandts, Memling, Vermeer, Velasquez, Goya, Metsu, Rubens, I was alone on a deserted island.

[18]

Chamber Music

If I stood further back, aimless dabs of color blended into forms, fading lines turned into space.

In Ferrières I waited a moment as I entered the *Salon des Tapisseries*. The sofa, deep enough to accommodate six, was covered by a soft fur. Sixteen plush down cushions, ranging from beige to purple in a delicate balance of shades, linked this voluptuous bed to the wall. And above hung a very large tapestry where centuries had faded the colors into soft pink and faint touches of blue. The tapestry represented an Oriental king on his throne under a tentlike dome, smoking a pipe that extended from his mouth to the ground. A couple of steps down and he was entertained by a young musician shaking a tambourine while performing on one foot while the other remained eternally in the air. Ladies surrounded him, a garden, some old ruins. Other tapestries covered the walls and were framed by heavy wood paneling. I stood facing a desk or, more exactly, a museum-piece table carved in the eighteenth century and decorated with heavy, intricate bronze moldings. On it stood a worn leather album full of signatures—German signatures. In 1870, the invading Germans had made their headquarters in the castle and the generals and officers residing or passing through signed the guest book, evidently considering themselves welcome guests, wanting to imprint the reality of their lives on eternity, maybe as a gift to the peaceful, ageless trees.

Around the chimney were large, wide armchairs covered with velvet, extending into the room and forming a convenient circle where friends could gather. Close to a warm, crackling fire, ladies sank into the soft down cushions, rings and bracelets dangling on their arms, their brocaded dresses blending with the red and green velvets. There was a fastidious abandon about their movements and yet with mellow enticing smiles and sensuous thrusts, they looked at the gentlemen standing around in tuxedos, leaning slightly in gestures of gallantry, as they searched for the right compliments.

As I silently shook everyone's hand, performing my only duty, the room filled with people. This gathering was different from the usual hunting party weekends. There was a man sitting at the piano, but the piano was covered with old richly brocaded velvet, photographs, art objects, a vase full of orchids. Yet the keys were uncovered and seemed about to come alive. Then I noticed two other men, one holding a violin, the other a cello. They seemed to appear from nowhere, or maybe they had been there all along. I couldn't tell. I gazed at the two delicate instruments. In this room, where every step touched invaluable old art pieces, I suddenly saw something really precious. The cello was deep red. Those three musicians were separate from the guests. They were not part of the help, and yet not part of the society. It was hard to understand, but they seemed suddenly part of my private world. The pianist hit a note; the violin and cello made small tuning sounds. There was a silence, a heaviness, a respect toward something unknown about to come, something great, something one should look up to, an insincere veneration of something that had not yet appeared.

They played. As I sat quietly among moving sounds, my mind wandered. I glared at the cello but didn't know why. The music was soft, it was loud, it was silent, it rushed me. I heard, but didn't listen. It was Nanny, it was arithmetic, it was long hours in the schoolroom, it was bicycling in the woods, it was torment, it was peace, it was a mood so full it was empty, it was mellow in a world where I was neither good nor bad. I was just lazy, in a fuzzy space. I kept glaring at the cello. Then it stopped. There was applause. My parents' guests went up to the musicians with sighs of admiration, everyone seeming to talk at the same time. "It was beautiful, it was great!" The musicians had become important. Every person smiled as they shook hands with each musician. I suddenly felt isolated. What had they heard that was bloating the atmosphere? My mother came to me and asked, "Did you like it?" There was awe in her voice, and I felt nothing. I knew there should be veneration in my answer, but there wasn't. I had spent time in some pleasant dream. Yes, I must be stupid. I couldn't remember a single melody. I looked at my mother. Could she sing one back? Then, in a loud voice I said, "I liked the cellist best!"

"Don't scream that!" She hushed me in great embarrass-ment.

II

The Obsession

[19]

Passion

Entering adolescence, I dreamt of love. The nature of an adolescent's dreams is determined by early childhood experiences. A child raised from birth with gentleness and tenderness will later incorporate those qualities in her sexual life. On the other hand, a child exposed to brutality associates love with violence and may become masochistic. I sensualized Nanny's cruelty, and therefore, my dreams of physical satisfaction were dreams of violence, of submission to sadism. Through adolescence my passions had magnified because I had been so suppressed and alone.

During that early start of adolescence, two important events marked a turning point in my development.

Mademoiselle was replaced by a new governess. The first day she made us feel comfortable. "You need not call me Mademoiselle; my name is Marcelle." She was a tall, healthy, open-hearted person. It did not take her long to understand the situation with Miss Swainston. Though she never spoke against her or even discussed her, I knew beyond the shadow of a doubt that she was siding with us, that she was a friend. But it took several years before she could establish an anchor strong enough to outroot Miss Swainston.

Then one day my mother said, "I found you a piano teacher, a really charming person."

"No," I immediately answered, "no more music for me, I am not gifted."

My mother continued, "She is a pupil of Alfred Cortot and she has a great reputation. If you don't have perfect pitch the violin is a bad choice. Piano will be more suitable for you."

I had failed so completely with music; I couldn't consider repeating such an experience. I revolted against putting more demands on myself which I couldn't live up to. I couldn't face more humiliations.

I looked at my mother and asked, "Must I really play piano?"

"Yes, I would like you to try once more. I know you will enjoy this teacher, but if after an honest try you don't like it, we will stop."

"All right," I agreed reluctantly. "When will she come?"

"Who?"

"The new piano teacher."

"She doesn't come. You go to her. Tomorrow is your first lesson."

"Oh." I was fearful but also pleased. This was a major change.

Yvonne Lefebure greeted us with warmth. "Please make yourself comfortable; I will be with you in a few minutes." She returned to the piano where a girl perhaps nine or ten years old sat ready to perform and played beautifully, with authority and ease.

Yvonne Lefebure was very short, under five feet, with extremely long blond hair that if not pinned up would have reached the floor. Her complexion, so clear and light, made her skin seem transparent. I felt immediately attracted to her sparkling way of teaching. She evoked in me a passionate desire to work. That was the second turning point in my life. I had an outlet, something to aim for. So I spent many hours at the piano. Though I had no natural ability for music, I started to improve, and the more I improved the harder I tried. With the attempt to express myself, I now had a purpose, so I hung on. I practiced and practiced.

Years ago I had fallen in love with Anna Pavlova and her performance of the "Dying Swan." I saw her only once, and in time my enthusiasm faded, though her image remained alive. So at the age of sixteen, when I was taken to hear the famous pianist Alfred Cortot, my dormant emotions had fermented and were ready to explode.

Cortot entered the stage, set off a burst of applause and I immediately fell under his magnetic power. He walked to the piano with a positive and controlled gait. Though he seemed reserved there was something dynamic about his personality. I was surprised to note a tremble in his hands as he struck the first chords. This was a Chopin recital, full of tenderness, with great sensitivity in the music.

I was ready for a crush, so right then I fell desperately in love with music, with Cortot, with my own need to open, to achieve. Before beginning Cortot waited a few seconds—intensely charged seconds in which the very room seemed caught in the grip of his concentration.

From the first measure an atmosphere was established. I followed Cortot through every mood and I was particularly impressed with his interpretation of the Second Prelude and wondered how a simple melody could give me such a cold, painful feeling, dark and sinister. When I listened, music never evoked pictures, so I was astonished to discover that in this Prelude Cortot saw "the far-off empty sea." Yes, the impassioned Eighth Prelude in F-sharp minor reached deep into my tormented heart, but the Prelude in B major was to reveal a new conception of life—one of charm and delicate warmth, not exactly the life I knew with Nanny. Cortot played the next Prelude, in G-sharp minor, with a trembling and nervous rhythm. Among these classics, one especially caught my heart—the Prelude in A-flat major. The happy and confident tenderness with which Cortot interpreted this Prelude awoke in me the idea of love. For the first time I thought how wonderful it would be to love deeply and be loved deeply in return.

The Preludes came to an end amid long and thunderous applause. I remained under the spell of the pieces and sat motionless. It was not until the maestro came back for the third time that I began to applaud.

I thought, "It's strange. I haven't the feeling he plays the piano but that he interprets human nature with a fine intensity and a thousand delicate colors, that he expresses emotions beyond my experience." I decided I wanted to work so that I, too, could express myself. This new impulse stimulated my concentration and kept my secret ambition alive for several years. I *had* to play well enough so that Cortot would listen to me—and I knew I would.

After that first concert my mother was surprised to find me in such a state of excitement. She remarked to my father, "It is not good for that child to stay up so late!"

"Mother can't understand," I thought disdainfully, keeping in mind that Alfred Cortot would play two days later. I was determined not to miss the concert.

That night after I heard him, I went to bed but couldn't sleep. Mulling over the events of the evening, I saw a path for the outlet of my confused feelings: a new world had opened up as I had heard a performance that with no hesitation I called masterly.

Excited, happy and impatient, I waited for the concert. This time Cortot played the F minor Concerto of Bach, conducting it as well. During this piece I thought the orchestra was too loud. For an encore he played the "Seguidilla" of Albeniz. Not my taste: colorful, yes, but without feeling. As he played I noticed that the fireworks of the piece clashed violently with the interpreter's beautiful head, with his profound and tormented expression. In the second half of the program he performed Debussy's "Children's Corner," but I was to receive an amazing shock: Cortot stopped in the middle of the "Petit Berger," a short, easy piece. He dropped his hands from the keyboard, murmured, "Pardon," waited an instant, then continued to play. For a moment his memory had gone blank. His face wore a look of such suffering that it made me tremble. I felt his anguish so keenly I couldn't even pity him: I suffered along with him.

After the concert I followed Mademoiselle Lefebure into the foyer. Cortot was putting on his cloak, trying to make his way through the thick crowd that besieged him. I sensed his effort to be polite as he shook hands with his admirers, and I watched him close the door of the elevator with a little relief; he wanted to be alone and I hoped he would find peace.

For a long time I was haunted by the memory of his sad face. I dreamed that he was spending long sleepless nights. What torments for one minute of forgetfulness!

As months passed, I gave more and more time to piano practice and to Alfred Cortot. I was not discouraged by my first
failures; I had decided to expend every effort. When I was tired
I thought of the maestro. I had to be worth his attention. I *had*
to reach him.

Several months passed without a Cortot concert. I played his
records—pale reproduction of his genius. I was giving up
school to spend hours each day at the piano.

"You ought not to neglect your studies completely," my
mother said, concerned by my obsessive behavior. "Spend one
or two hours a day reading," she urged, "develop yourself outside of piano. That would be more sensible."

Instead of giving me much-needed encouragement, she tried
to hold me back. As she spoke something inside me protested;
her attitude provoked in me a feeling of obstinacy. I wanted to
know Cortot, and when I noticed a small improvement in my
work I dared to face my secret desire.

One morning I approached my mother: "Do you think it
would be possible for me to meet Cortot some day?"

The question which had been burning was finally out. As the
answer was evasive, I kept on asking even my mother's friends.

"I do wish you would introduce me! Am I so indiscreet—?"

"Not at all, it's very easy. I'll arrange it for you," I heard
time and again. But no one did arrange it.

I never missed an opportunity to hear Cortot. I went to all
his concerts and lectures on interpretation. I became more and
more enthusiastic as my admiration for him grew. I managed
to be in Paris each time he gave a concert. The obsession with
Alfred Cortot was growing. Any time away from the world of
Cortot seemed wasted. Riding, golf, even chess could not compete with my feelings for Cortot.

My mother continued to be annoyed at my one-track mind.
She wanted to pull me out of myself and announced one day
that she and my father were going to take a trip to the North
African desert and that I should go with them. So we packed
into a car with a chauffeur. I sat between my mother and father. Another car followed us with a maid, a valet, trunks and
suitcases, and behind them, still another car with food. This
caravan set out on a trail in the sandy desert, headed for an
oasis that we were to reach ten hours later. Because of the con-

fined monotony of the drive, or simply because of bad luck, I
started to catch a cold and started to cough. I coughed and
coughed until I was aching and my insides seemed torn. My
father said, "Let's stop and eat something." The chauffeur was
told to motion to the cars behind. But the two cars had vanished! We were astonished, bewildered. What could have happened? The chauffeur volunteered, "Maybe they didn't notice
when we stopped at the last turn and got ahead of us. They
must think they lost us and are speeding to catch up." So off
we went, chasing them as they were chasing us. "Stupid, cre-
tins, how can one be so dumb?" growled my father. Frustration
and anger were mounting on each side of me as coughing made
my chest more and more sore. We drove on and on. I was fearful. Would I ever get anything to drink? Suddenly we saw both
cars, stopped and waiting. They had finally realized that something was wrong.

When we reached a town in the oasis that evening I went to
bed with fever and acute bronchitis. My parents located a doctor who gave me some triangular lozenges that helped the
cough. When I recovered I started to be drawn to the rocky,
dry, lifeless roads as we traveled for long hours across the desert. I began to stare at a dark spot on the horizon until slowly
each palm tree became clearly defined and the oasis came to
life. Even though this fascinated me, Cortot was still dominating my thoughts and I was anxious to get back to the piano. I
knew Cortot was to give an evening of trios with Thibaud and
Casals in Paris. We passed Laghouat, Ghardaïa and finally
stopped at Biskra. From there my parents had planned to return home. I was excited with the prospect of Cortot's next
concert when my parents suggested we go on to El Goléa. If we
went, I would miss the concert.

"No," I murmured, "that is not possible. I *have* to be back."
Going to El Goléa would have meant backtracking, so when I
begged and nagged my mother she agreed to go home. He will
never know that I cut short a beautiful trip because of him, I
thought as we left the desert.

When I got back to Paris I returned to the same routine for a
year, practicing several hours a day and obsessed more and
more by the necessity to meet Cortot. I wanted to tell him, "No

one else in the world plays like you do." But would he be interested? No matter: my feelings were stronger than any logic.

As the months passed, I tormented everyone and still could not reach the maestro. Then I made the decision to approach him after his next concert.

Cortot had just played the Chausson "Concert" with Jacques Thibaud. Very much moved, I went toward the green room backstage. I stopped for a few moments at the door, amazed to find myself in a nearly empty room. In a corner three or four women were flirting with Thibaud. Cortot was alone. I watched him from a distance and froze.

"Go to him," I told myself, "shake hands . . . tell him . . . it is easy . . . yes, I so much want him to know."

I took a few steps and then, with decided gesture, extended my hand. I told Cortot quite spontaneously what was in my heart. "No one in the world plays as you do." He bowed slightly and said, "Thank you." I had the impression that he was trying to remember who I was.

[20]

A Marriage

It was true that I played better chess than Bethsabée and I was good at golf and also was better at the piano, but on the other hand, she was getting ahead in the schoolroom. As I was spending hours practicing piano, she announced that she was going to pass her baccalaureate. This hit me. I was seventeen and totally uneducated, living in a dream world of passion for the piano, for music, for Alfred Cortot, for golf, for chess, a dream world of passion for love, for sex, while my quiet little sister was getting a real education. She would be out in the world, equal with other boys and girls. She was going to pass her *"bashot."* She was intelligent. "Yes, I thought, she has blue eyes like my father. She has his intelligence."

"Girls need not learn," my father had said over and over again. Then why was he so proud of Bethsabée?

My mother enjoyed her extensive social life and suffered as she watched me become more and more withdrawn and limited to the piano. I would have liked to be more accepted by friends, especially by boys. I wished I could flirt, but I was unable to. Boys didn't look at me. Once again my mother didn't understand. Instead of helping, she tried to incorporate me into her own social life.

"I am giving a dinner next Thursday," she said.

"I can't be there," was my immediate reaction. "Cortot is

conducting one of his private concerts at the School of Applied Arts."

"But you're not going!"

"Of course I am."

"That is absolutely ridiculous. You're unable to miss one concert. You can't stay a week in the mountains when Cortot is in Paris. You spend all your days at the piano for this man. You can't even take a quiet trip because of Alfred Cortot, old enough to be your grandfather. I've had enough. You are going to stop this nonsense."

I tried to avoid speaking of it, but I couldn't help thinking. How could I have forced myself to work if I hadn't had Cortot for inspiration, if I hadn't had the hope of one day being worthy of his attention? I could scarcely conceive of this possibility. I was sinking. As Cortot seemed unreachable, my thoughts drifted toward marriage. Coming straight from the nursery, I didn't associate marriage with love. Love was for Cortot. But I was ready to accept in marriage anyone who would be kind to me.

Neither did I associate sex with love. Of course, sex during the post-Victorian epoch was enveloped in a kind of mysterious aura. Talking about sex was taboo, yet it was on everyone's mind. Jokes, accompanied by an understanding giggle, were numerous. Sex was dangerous, it was forbidden, it was envied. There was a whole society of women who were free to accommodate the men. They were far above ordinary whores and were called *le demi-monde*, the half-world, in opposition to *la femme du monde*, the society lady. A society lady would never speak to a woman from the "half-world." But she was quick to recognize one in a public place. "Oh, look, there's the famous Marie; she's very high-class."

Wives worried. This half-world was very attractive, always friendly and ready to please. A double life was common. Men spent an hour here and there before coming home, or kept an apartment on the side.

But my parents believed marriage was the right thing for me to enter into, so one day my mother came to me and said, "It is time for you to get married."

"Yes," I answered, "but I don't know anyone."

"I'll introduce you to a distant cousin; his name is Robert Calmann-Levy. He and his brother own the Calmann-Levy Publishing Company. I haven't met him, but people say he is charming."

So I was introduced to a man a little shorter than myself, with a round face and a monotonous voice. He lacks life, I decided, as I wasn't attracted to him; however, the idea of marriage *was* attractive, so I saw him two or three times. Though we were strangers, he complied with expectations and asked me to marry him. This was a new experience, a success in a way, an opening to the unknown world. But what should I do? I wondered. I went to my mother. "He asked me to marry him; what should I do?"

"I don't know—ask your father."

I went to my father. He was sitting at his dressing table, shaving with an open razor blade. I sat down, watched him quietly for a few minutes as he stretched the skin over his bony face. "Calmann-Levy asked me to marry him; what should I do?"

He turned a smile toward me and said, "*Ma cocotte*, that is very nice, but I don't know, go and ask your mother," and he kept on shaving.

I went upstairs slowly, knocked on Guy's door, and blurted out, "Should I get married? He asked me."

"Well," Guy said, "I don't know, let's talk about it. Do you like him?"

"I don't know—I have seen him so little."

"Do you want to get married?"

"Yes."

"Then go ahead," he said. Unfortunately, my brother did not know how to cope with life any more than I did. A few years later, in a similar way, he married a woman my mother had picked out for him and he, too, was unhappy.

But once decided, I looked forward to getting married. It didn't really matter who my husband was, I told myself; I would respond to affection.

In my dreams though Cortot was love, marriage was life. Marriage meant escaping from the fortress of my childhood. A strong relationship in marriage could wipe out Cortot.

About two weeks after my engagement, my mother came to me one evening and said, "Mrs. D. is giving a dinner and you are invited." I waited. "When you were so anxious to meet Cortot I had mentioned it to her. He will be there Thursday evening." This was so unexpected that I was stunned into silence.

"Are you pleased?"

"Oh, yes," I murmured.

My mother loved to choose elegant clothes, and I barely suppressed a bad mood at the endless fittings. Preparation for the wedding continued but the wedding took a second place in my inner world as I counted the days until I would meet Cortot. Tuesday—Wednesday—Thursday—a dream was about to come true.

Several guests were already at the dinner when I arrived but not Cortot. Nine o'clock, he is late! I thought. I watched the door as if hypnotized. When it opened, my heartbeat became louder. But only a small gentleman, fat and bald, marched in, a large smile on his round face. My disappointment mixed with fear: suppose Cortot didn't come! But at that very moment I saw him enter, preceded by his wife. The hostess introduced him to various people, and when my turn came he looked directly at me and said, "I have seen you—at school?" At dinner he sat next to my mother, and I sat opposite them. Luckily the table was narrow. Suddenly he leaned across and asked, "Do you practice a lot?"

"As much as I can; I started piano very late."

After dinner I stayed near him. He talked of the school, of the different pupils, of various courses.

Robert, my fiancé, came up and said to him, "Your picture is all over the house."

"I am touched—very touched," he answered, with a slight bow of his head. Then he congratulated me on my engagement. Shortly after that he left in his black automobile with a red stripe. This was the last time I saw Cortot before my marriage.

The wedding day came. I wore the traditional long white dress, though I have no recollection of what it looked like, nor do I remember walking down the synagogue aisle with my father. But I do remember standing after the ceremony, shaking hands for many hours. When the guests thinned out late in the evening I was numb from exhaustion, my feet were sore and I was aching all over. In that tense and tired condition I left with a new husband, a stranger, on a train heading for the south of France. I sat on the lower berth of the compartment; but instead of joy and excitement, I experienced an immense letdown. Tears rolled down my cheeks. I cried and cried without feeling any relief. When Robert asked me why I was crying I answered, "I don't know, I really don't know." I was embarrassed, but it didn't seem to bother him. With an immense effort, as in my growing-up years with Miss Swainston, I pulled myself together and allowed him to consummate the marriage.

Our honeymoon surroundings were rich with possibilities—Cannes, the beach, a beautiful blue ocean, a casino, gambling. I was free, I had a husband, it was *my* honeymoon. But Robert spent little time with me, and many evenings, sensing something was wrong, I waited alone in the hotel.

My parents were happy to see me get married. In their minds, I was doing the right thing. For Robert, our marriage was a successful business deal. For me, it was an escape, an attempt to grow up. Although I was hoping for understanding, for closeness, what I really wanted most out of marriage was children.

This was my honeymoon, but it bore no resemblance to a real honeymoon. I accompanied Robert to the casino and tried gambling. Sometimes I settled myself with 1,000 francs at a ten-franc baccarat table, and as soon as I got a little ahead I stopped. Every night my thousand francs increased until I had doubled it. Then one night I started off by losing and lost without ever getting ahead until my profit had dissolved, and even my initial 1,000 francs. I went home so frustrated that I never tried gambling again, a lucky decision, as there had been gambling in the family.

My father's sister, Beatrice Ephrussi, whom we called Auntie Bea, had been introduced to gambling by her husband. They played poker compulsively until she lost most of her fortune. Aunt Beatrice was bony, thin, and nervous, with very long white hair. Apparently her hair had turned completely white at the age of eighteen. I was told she had been incredibly beautiful. Someone compared her hair to snow on an orange tree. She was without children, and for pets she kept two very small completely blue frogs that she loved. They were always in a little glass bowl on her night table. When she died, the butler who had been with her for uncounted years went to the funeral carrying the bowl with her two little blue frogs. It was in Aunt Beatrice's house, 19 Avenue Foch, where I lived alone after I divorced Calmann-Levy, and it was also in that house that I first entertained Grisha, my future husband. It was in Aunt Beatrice's house that my parents lived on their return from America after the Second World War. Their palace on rue St. Florentin overlooking the Place de la Concorde had been confiscated by the Vichy Government. Later I inherited Aunt Beatrice's house and eventually I sold it.

The first week of my honeymoon passed, and after my gambling loss I shared nothing with Robert. He didn't encourage sharing or becoming close; on the contrary, he made me feel unneeded, even unwanted. Sex relations must have been fairly insignificant to me, as I cannot remember that part of my honeymoon. Of course, I didn't know at the time that his mistress had followed him to Cannes. But without realizing it, I sensed that I was in the way, so I suggested we go to Arcachon and visit my parents.

"Oh, no," he answered, "there's no reason to leave. It's very nice here."

"I would like to leave," I insisted, "let's go."

"No, I want to stay here." Robert stared at his feet in silence. I continued, "Well, I'm going."

"I am not."

"Then I will go alone."

"You wouldn't do that!"

"I will if you refuse to come with me."

"Really?"

"Yes."

"Are you sure?"

"Absolutely."

After a short hesitation, he said, "All right, I guess I'll join you very soon." Actually he was glad to see me leave, but for appearances he raised a few mild objections.

If my parents found it strange that I came home alone from my honeymoon they didn't show it, and the rest of the summer rolled by at Arcachon as if nothing had happened.

[21]

Back to the Old Life

I think Robert joined me in Arcachon with my parents before the end of the summer, though I don't remember it, nor do I remember my feelings when we got back together.

After the summer my parents settled us in an apartment in the palace rue St. Florentin where I was raised. It was a small apartment with a separate entrance. From the window I couldn't see the Place de la Concorde nor the Jardin des Tuileries as I had in my childhood, as the apartment looked out on the entrance yard. Our life was somewhat patterned on the past. We had a cook; Robert's valet also served at the table. I was lucky to have Renée Ovise as a maid, a support, and a friend. But my inner turmoil hadn't changed. I still felt the burning desire to express myself, to love, to excel, to show the world, to have children. I wanted *so* badly to have my own little ones, but none came.

Nothing had really changed in my life. I was still alone, practicing piano and thinking of Cortot.

In an attempt to become part of the outside world, I turned toward my old interest and went to a chess club, only to face another humiliation. I took a board in a simultaneous exhibition. When I reached a critical position I must have shown anxiety and fear, for a stranger behind me said, "Move here." I followed his advice, and won the game. At the end the Grand Master said, pointing at me, "She played a good game."

My son Joram with his wife and two boys, Auran and Anton.

The last time we were all four together in April, 1976.

A Kiwi bird I made in 1985.

A sculpture: Infinity. In translucent alabaster.

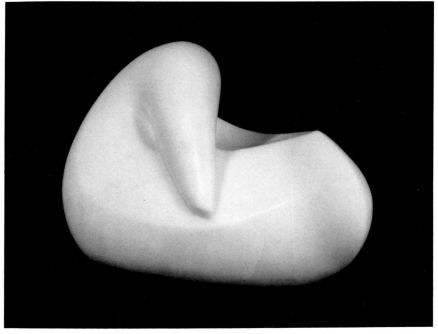

The very first stone I made entirely alone on which I struggled for a year before I met a teacher.

Grisha and I in 1938 in
Stamford, Connecticut.

My husband and I.

My husband with Jephta and Joram and the cello.

My husband and I with my bassoon. In the background the photo of Franklin Roosevelt was dedicated to my husband and framed with wood from the White House roof erected in 1817 and renovated in 1927.

My husband with Jephta and her three boys, Jonathan, Evan, and Eric.

Me (left) Pnina Salzman (a young pianist from Israel) and Alfred Cortot.

Grisha (Gregor Piatigorsky). The first picture he gave me.

My grandmother in front of one of her paintings.

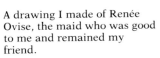

A drawing I made of Renée Ovise, the maid who was good to me and remained my friend.

Ferrières—an outside view of the castle where I was raised.

My father, brother, and mother during the war.

Ferrières—one corner of the Salon des Tapisseries.

Ferrières—the lake where I saw ducks and swans.

"I helped her," the man said. Though he had shown me only one move, I felt ashamed. I arranged for the Grand Master to come and give me lessons. He came two or three times and I improved.

As my actual life seemed like an unfulfilled dream, my inner dream, the mirage, seemed to become more real. Cortot was not anymore a figure on the stage. I had met him, spoken to him and ached to see him again, but how? I had no friends and Robert was seldom there. Two years went by. I was practicing piano several hours a day, intensely and with confused feelings. Even though my experience in life was nonexistent, I knew something was really wrong. So I went to my father, told him that my marriage was not working out, and suggested a separation. He said that maybe I would be happier if we had an apartment outside of the building where I was raised. So my mother found a beautiful two-story apartment. I turned the upper floor into a music studio with two pianos. It was my own place and I felt relieved.

One day Artur Rubinstein, who was a close friend of my mother's when I was young, came to visit at the studio. I had never considered him any other way than as a friend of my mother's. From time to time he spoke to me, but he was intensely concentrated on himself. Once, I tried to compose a sonata and I mentioned it to him, hoping for encouragement or possibly even a little help. But he ridiculed me. "You know nothing about composition."

"I could try," I ventured shyly.

"Look," he said, "I know that a dress has a neck opening and two sleeves, but it does not mean that I could make a dress!"

"No," I said sadly, and gave up composing until years later when I was married to Gregor Piatigorsky. Then I wrote a small piece under the name "Paul Ari" and Grisha played it in several concerts.

Rubinstein and I had tea, and sat talking. I confessed how poorly my marriage was working out.

"Is there someone else?" Rubinstein asked.

"Yes, I do love someone else, but it is crazy." He was quiet. I continued, "He happens to be a musician, but he is very much older than I . . ." Silence. "I think you know him."

He perked up; his expression showed some interest. Then,

changing the subject, he spoke about his concerts, his successes, his glory.

I came back to my problem. "You know him," I repeated. "Maybe you have guessed who he is?"

"No, I haven't," he said, and he got up as if ready to leave.

"I'm sure you know," I insisted as I followed him to the door.

"No, really." He turned, looked at me, his bulging eyes seeming to say, "Tell me." He repeated, "No," with a slight hesitation.

Finally I said, "Alfred Cortot."

His expression shrank, as if he had been slapped in the face. He said good-bye nicely. Shortly after, I heard that he married a young Polish woman, Nela, with whom he had four children. The possibility of considering him other than my mother's friend would never have entered my head. Conversely, the possibility of someone not being in love with him would never have entered *his* head. What a misunderstanding!

[22]

Cortot Notices Me

It was Cortot who had given me both the desire and the means to achieve. And now I wanted to see him, to thank him again. I needed his presence, I hoped to be worthy of his smile, to be worthy of a word of encouragement. I stared at his photograph as if to fill myself with his magnetism.

One day as I was staring a happy thought occurred: a manuscript. Cortot was a collector—that I knew from hearsay. If I could find him an excellent one, one that would interest him, he would want to see it! I immediately began to look for a manuscript. I received word from Berlin, they had a wonderful proposition: the manuscript of the First Ballade of Chopin. It was very expensive—60,000 francs. A lot of money. But the possibility of letting such an opportunity escape was out of the question.

Eight days later I unwrapped the precious package. Carefully, I turned the pages covered with Chopin's fine script. Once more I thanked the maestro for having unconsciously shown me a new interest in life. This beautiful manuscript could be the beginning of a fine collection.

I asked my mother to invite Cortot for dinner. She yawned. I urged her to the library where I sat her at the desk, put a pen in her hand, and told her, "Write at once or else you will never do it. He is playing on the nineteenth. We'd have to ask him for one of the days after the concert." Fatigue added to her desire to please me, so she wrote the invitation.

The answer was not long in arriving and the date of the dinner was fixed. I could begin to live. It would be the start, but the start of what? Of a marvelous idyll? I didn't know real love but could one love from a distance?

It occurred to me that the personality of the man might not correspond to that of the artist. I immediately saw the absurdity of such a question; there can't be such a split. The artist reflects the man. With contradictory feelings I waited, counting the hours.

The moment came. Cortot was standing beside me. I drank in his every word. Without waiting for dinner, I ventured the burning question in a hesitant voice.

"When you made your edition of the Ballades, had you seen the manuscript?"

He didn't answer immediately. Then, to my relief, he said, "I had not seen them all."

"The Ballade in G minor?"

"No, but the Second."

"Yes, that is in the conservatory," I said; "But," I triumphed at last, "I have the manuscript of the First Ballade."

Cortot expressed mild astonishment. As he remained silent I continued. "Would it interest you to see it?"

"Oh, definitely," he said without hesitating, then asked, "Now?"

"Now is a little inconvenient; but any day you wish to come to my house, I will be happy to show it to you." (Actually, the manuscript was in the drawer of the table on which I was leaning.)

"May I phone you to make an appointment—perhaps Thursday morning?"

The evening wore on. We played bridge, I even won ninety francs from him, and as he left he said, "I will call you Thursday at noon."

At twenty minutes to twelve the phone rang. It was Cortot, and our rendezvous was set for Friday, the next day, at two.

Robert had come down with the flu and I couldn't help hoping he would get worse and be obliged to stay in his room. If one wished strongly enough for something, would that make it come true? The next morning, when I timidly went to see Robert, I could scarcely conceal my joy: he was heavily covered and told me he had 102 degrees of fever, expressing his regret that he had to stay in bed.

Alone! I would be alone with the maestro. We would have a tête-à-tête. In a few hours he would be in my drawing room with me. He would talk to me. He would not be far away as in a concert hall where I could only watch him, nor in a salon where I couldn't compete with the other women around him. But I was too excited to be completely happy.

I sat at the piano. To control my expectations I slowly played the D minor scale. I was still playing when the servant opened the door and stepped back to allow Cortot to enter.

I shall never forget that moment, the moment I had lived so many times in my imagination. My mind had created an unreachable genius, and here he stood, alone, with me, a simple and friendly older man, his hair slightly long, almost falling onto his forehead. Embarrassment made me feel weak and clumsy. Had he noticed my lack of poise? I wondered.

Cortot held out both hands, saying, "Goo—good!" The realization of my dreams was overwhelming. Unfortunately, I was neither sophisticated nor cunning. I didn't know how to create a warm atmosphere. I found nothing to say. Did I seem cold and distant, in a dreadful contrast to my true feelings? Fear made me brusque and I prayed he would somehow feel the importance of his presence. How I wished he could realize what I couldn't convey!

Cortot seemed interested in the manuscript. He noted several differences from the published version and made notes of those variations.

"May I come back this spring to take some notes?" The offer was so casual it caught me unaware. I was awkward and too slow to understand that luck was offering me what I dreamed of getting. I wanted to say, "That would be wonderful!" Instead, I silently held out the facsimile of the manuscript. He hesitated.

"I've had it made for you."

"I'm touched—very touched." He moved his head to the side

and smiled, in an attempt to be less formal. "You must write
something on it."

With an exclamation I showed my embarrassment. "But
what could I write?"

He said immediately: "To Alfred Cortot, in mutual love for
Chopin."

He had spoken very low. The simplicity and purity of his
voice went straight to my heart. I sat, pen in hand. I looked at
him walking up and down. His inscription didn't suit me, as I
wanted to write something more personal, but at the time I
couldn't think of another. Discouraged, I asked him what he
had said. He repeated the inscription in a more assured tone.

After looking over the manuscript, Cortot sat down silently,
before the fire. The silence grew; it lasted for several minutes
whereupon he suggested I play for him. The prospect was
frightening. I would have preferred to wait for another time
when I could be further advanced. But playing was preferable
to this silence.

He made me play the first page of his exercise book in order
to show me the exact movement. He put his left arm about my
chair. I shivered, feeling him so near, and for a moment I had a
wild desire to fall into his arms, to tell him everything. But I
couldn't.

"Do you practice this?" he asked, pointing to a score of the
Bach Italian Concerto which he had found on the piano.

"Yes, but I don't know it well. It's too difficult for me."

"That makes no difference. Play it for me." I apologized for
the mediocrity of my playing. He promised to be indulgent and
I attacked the first chord with all the authority I could muster.
When I finished he explained certain passages by playing them
for me and then he asked me to do it again. I had a certain gift
for imitation and the maestro said smilingly, "You're a very
good pupil!"

He pointed out several parts and promised he would hear me
again in a little while. The difficulty of these works terrified
me: two Chopin Études, the First Ballade, and the F minor
Concerto of Bach.

He paid me the only compliment that could touch me: "You
play much less amateurishly than I would have believed." This
phrase went to my heart like a stimulant.

As he was about to leave, I realized what a marvelous and yet frustrating hour I had just spent. I watched him walk toward the elevator. He waved before closing the door. I stood gazing down the hall, an empty pit in my stomach. It was over.

Cortot had promised to hear me again! Did he mean it?

I practiced desperately. I thought only of Cortot. Sometimes I remembered a concert, an expression, a gesture, a phrase. But I seemed to be living in the past with no hope for the future: an unfortunate state. Without growth one shrinks.

After each concert I went backstage. Like everyone else, I stood in line to shake his hand. Then, in a corner, I waited. Little by little the foyer emptied and still I waited just to see him get in the car with his wife. From the faint light of his cigarette I could see his face. Then I walked home, and to delay facing my husband, I went to have supper with my mother.

It seemed that every moment of my life depended on Cortot. If he seemed tired, I worried; when he didn't play as well as usual, I felt him suffer and I suffered too. Often he seemed preoccupied and anxious, and I was depressed at not being able to share his troubles. I thought too many people worshiped him, deified him, but no one understood him; he never relaxed, he never confided. But at other times I thought my judgment was unfounded, as I saw him only in public. But it was plain to me that happiness was not possible with his sensitive nature. He seemed to miss something. Could it be youth? Did he think himself old?

One evening Robert tried to communicate. "What are you thinking about?" He had been watching me for a while.

"Nothing."

"Have you deep worries?"

"No, why?"

"Are you ill?"

"On the contrary; I am very well." I was annoyed that Robert was suddenly trying to enter my world.

"It's not nice to answer me that way. I love you, you know. Please feel you can talk to me. I'm discreet, I understand." I sensed insincerity.

"I assure you I have nothing to say!"

The truth was that I had not succeeded in putting Cortot out of my mind. I was held as in a powerful dream, glued to a fiction. But could a fiction make me grow? Is love a fiction? I was richer for having a great passion, but the price was high. I was gnawing at myself. Love needs an exchange to flourish; but each act of mine, each thought of mine, each emotion reached out to an unreachable figure. If only he knew! Would he really be touched by my feelings? I doubted it. I was overwhelmed by my own passion, to the point of suffocation. "He must know," I murmured, "he must know—maybe I could write to him." I imagined expressing my feelings on a cold white sheet of paper and immediately rejected the idea as absurd. Maybe I could ask Mademoiselle Lefebure to speak to him. But that seemed no good. I decided such strong emotion could only be conveyed personally. Cortot would understand me only by direct contact—a look, an expression that would show him my love more than any written words.

[23]

Still Chasing

I learned the Chopin "Barcarolle" and went to Cortot's house alone. It was our second meeting in private. He received me upstairs in his small studio, and he remained a polite teacher.

"Considerable progress," he remarked. I was intimidated, and dared not change the atmosphere.

Cortot accompanied me out to the elevator. I was frustrated not to have made the best of this meeting. Agitated, I shook my head: I have no experience, I thought, I lack feminine intuition. Next time—but *will* there be a next time? The future seemed like an empty corridor, hopelessly dark.

Robert never came on vacation with me. He claimed he wasn't able to leave his work so as summer came I left the city and my problems for the fresh air of Normandy. Bethsabée and I loved the simplicity and absence of luxury, no telephone, no electricity. We enjoyed the soft light of candles. It was a happy atmosphere in Touques, the little village where we stayed. The Maison Blanche was in the fields with the baby horses cantering behind their mothers.

"One can work here, don't you think?" Bethsabée said.

I stood near the window, watching the horses in the fields. Gazing at the flowers, the sun, the birds, all so full of life, the urge of youth slowly returned. I wanted to run carefree in the fields with the horses. I turned to my sister as if to escape

temptation and said, "Cortot suggested I practice the First
Ballade of Chopin this summer."

I put myself on a rigorous schedule. For several days I did
nothing but practice the piano. But thoughts of Cortot began to
obsess me once more. I wondered if he were still in Paris. I'd
heard nothing of him for three months and imagined he could
be sick and I wouldn't know it. I found a telephone in town and
started dialing: Trocadero 31 42. Ten minutes to wait. (At that
time there was a wait for any long-distance call.) I patiently
smoked a cigarette. A woman's voice answered, "Monsieur Cortot has just gone out." I was lucky. Had he answered the phone
I could never have explained why I was calling and the embarrassment would have been crushing.

"Is he leaving soon for Saint-Cast?" I spoke decisively and
the person on the other end of the wire, taken unaware, answered, "Yes, but not until the first of the week. Who is calling?"

"It doesn't matter. Thank you, Madame."

The voice insisted. "Who is calling?" I hung up.

Saint-Cast was not far. I knew I shouldn't follow every impulse, but temptation grew, while reason said no. He may say:
"There is that woman again," I told myself. I wondered if I
should expose myself to humiliation. Although I was torn, I
convinced myself it would be all right to take a little trip to the
shores of Brittany and stop at Cortot's just to say hello. I said
to myself, "I will see if he is well. I will see his home—how he
lives."

I telephoned once again that evening, this time to my husband in Paris, to tell him my plans. He saw through my pretext
at once. Robert wouldn't allow me to make him ridiculous by
running after Cortot. He protested. I insisted, promising to take
Bethsabée along. After much discussion Robert reluctantly
gave in, complaining, "You never want to take a trip with me
for it is said 'Madame does not care for the automobile,' but
when it is a question of seeing your dear Cortot, you don't hesitate."

We set out the next morning and had traveled half the way
by noon. As I wanted to drive, my sister sat beside me and the
chauffeur took the back seat. We had been driving for about an

hour when Bethsabée said, "Why don't we stop for lunch? We should get to Saint-Cast in a couple of hours." Suddenly the realization that I should impose on Cortot made me nervous. I was torn between the compulsion to go and the knowledge that I shouldn't. So as I entered a turn going downhill, I took the wrong angle. We skidded and overturned. If I died he would never know—that thought flashed through my mind. Then I saw Bethsabée. "I'm all right," she volunteered as she quickly jumped out of the window.

Gasoline poured out of the gas tank, flooding the street with a strong smell. "Look out for fire!" said the chauffeur. "Don't smoke." He climbed out of the window and so did I. Luckily, there was no fire.

Dazed, I stood in the middle of the road, staring at the damaged Citroën and wondering by what miracle we had escaped unhurt. Only then was I truly afraid. I was seized with remorse. What if something had happened to my sister?

Bethsabée and I sat by the side of the road as the chauffeur went to get help. I reached in my briefcase for my old friend and security, the chess set, and there, sitting at the side of the road beside the overturned Citroën, we played chess.

I didn't see Cortot for the rest of the summer and discovered on my return to Paris that I even liked the heat of the city—the smells, the noise, the bustle. I would live again. Naturally, I hurried to his school and questioned the concierge.

"Monsieur Cortot comes in from time to time. He came the day before yesterday." This answer removed a terrible weight from my mind. What a relief! Though no concerts were announced, he was in the same city with me.

Time passed and I hadn't yet seen him. It was the day before the opening of school. A brilliant sun shed its hot rays on the earth and seemed to accent the noise and the smell of the cars. What's the use; fate is against me, I decided. But the thought of Cortot returning to school reawakened my desire.

I went to the school with an inner tightness. From the distance I saw a parked car—his car. I began to walk up and down before the entrance of the school. After ten minutes I gave up and questioned the maestro's chauffeur. At first he hesitated, then said, "Monsieur Cortot should come out at four-fifteen."

I sat down on a bench across the street and waited. I waited for an hour and a half. The chauffeur took pity, and when he finally saw the maestro he made a sign. I got up, went to him decisively, pretending I had just arrived. He seemed surprised. His first instinct was to ask me the reason for my visit to the school, but apparently he thought better of it. After an exchange of banal remarks about the summer he asked when he could hear me play. He was amiable, but as always his amiability seemed a bit forced. After a few minutes he shook hands, a distant smile on his face, full of a devilish charm. The car was off.

"How polite he is!" I sighed. "But how hurried he was. In his mind I do not exist."

[24]

First Attempt to Escape

Before I knew Cortot, I had been indifferent, even negligent, about clothes, to the despair of my mother. I went to the dressmaker only when absolutely necessary, often forgetting the appointments for fittings. With a sigh, my mother would try to adjust my scarf more elegantly or would push back a lock of disorderly hair. Now, wanting desperately to please, I tried to be more feminine. Time and again I returned to the couturier to match a difficult color. But my efforts were useless. Cortot noticed nothing; I was not attractive to him.

During this dark period a friend of my mother's, a very intelligent woman, came to tea. Her only son had been killed in the war. Such a loss was so painful that she turned to psychoanalysis for help. I immediately asked more about it. She gave me a name and I went to see the doctor. So I began analysis, which I believe contributed to my eventual maturing. My relationship with Robert was increasingly tense as I became more aware and my thoughts became more realistic. My teenage passion was attempting to become more concrete. I was trying to turn a mirage into reality. Psychoanalysis made me understand that I was creating my own problems instead of solving them. It was nice to have someone to speak to, but changes were up to me.

Some months later I was going to Cortot once more to play

part of the Schumann "Carnaval." As it was much too difficult,
I played it badly.

It was now up to me to create a more personal exchange on a
human level. When I finished playing I looked up at Cortot. I
felt close to him. Generally he was surrounded by a crowd, a
swarm of vultures. In this rather barren little room, the piano
with a picture of Chopin on it, some books, a collection of old
snuffboxes, a picture on an easel—all these objects lent an air
of unostentatious attractiveness. Seated quietly beside me, he
remained a teacher, his expression an impenetrable mask.
Abruptly, I turned to him.

"You said the other day that one can achieve anything with
willpower."

"Yes."

"Is that how one becomes happy?"

He seemed amazed and lowered his voice. For the first time
he spoke to me more naturally, and for a few minutes dropped
his reserve. Returning to the subject nearest my heart, I continued: "Love is never reciprocated!" I waited, but as he didn't
answer I didn't pursue the subject. There can be no doubt, I
decided, Cortot does not want my love. The possibility of
seeing him in public scarcely consoled me. I was overstimu-
lated, haunted by the image I had created. One more opportunity of meeting him, of shaking hands with him, was the
center of my life. I was dependent on his moods; his fascinating
smile, his voice as its deep tones penetrated me. When he re-
sumed his distant manner I was even further magnetized.

When I had married Calmann-Levy a secretary was engaged
to pay the bills and do the accounting. I took for granted that
all the expenses were paid and kept in order, and as I never
looked at the books I didn't notice that Robert was keeping his
mistress in luxury with my funds. (I was not curious about his
private life because I was lost in my own inner world.) Though
Robert had no feelings for me, he didn't want to lose me. He
continued his double standard of life, thinking he could keep
me indefinitely on ice.

I knew we had nothing in common, but I now think that if he
had been sensitive to me I would have opened up to him and

my adolescent passion for Alfred Cortot would have crumbled. But as I became more aware of our problems, the more annoyed Robert got.

"After all, I didn't marry a schoolgirl," he complained. "I want a wife who busies herself at home."

"Who gets up at noon and thrives on cocktail parties," I finished. I stopped short, starting to wonder if maybe it was partly my fault that we didn't get along. I was angry at myself for doubting and I wanted to be nice but in vain I sought a warm word. I may have married Robert thinking of Cortot, but maybe underneath I was secretly hoping Robert would win me over by compassion.

"I feel friendly toward you," I stammered with an effort. I tried to convey to him that our quarrel had nothing to do with Cortot. I went on. "But we are not really meant for each other. We are too dissimilar, we will never be able to understand each other."

Although the friction between Robert and me wasn't entirely caused by Cortot, I knew my strong feelings for Cortot didn't help.

On the other hand, I lacked the willpower to stop seeing Cortot. I continued to attend his performances, after which I quickly went straight to my bedroom and closed the door so that I could be alone. (Robert and I had separate bedrooms.) Alone I could think, I could be a person, I could be myself as in years past, deep in the sand on the beach, my feet in muddy salt water. I would, however, say good night to Robert before going to bed. We had no more sexual relations and I had given up the hope of having children. As he felt me slipping away, he sometimes came to my room and paced the floor. The heavy silence was filled with reproaches reflecting his anger. Then we quarreled.

Usually, Robert never came home before nine or nine-thirty at night. "Why do you stay out so late?" I asked, "Maybe you could think of me a little too!"

"I'm working."

"Not that late."

"Yes, I am working; don't nag me," he said, and then as I started to ask for more consideration, the tension mounted.

Without consulting me, Robert had bought a country place three hours from Paris where he spent most of his weekends. Sometimes he asked politely if I wanted to go. I wasn't anxious to leave my practicing, and he never insisted. I was getting more and more restless and more aware how wrong my life was. So one day I said, "I think we should separate for a while."

He looked at me, surprised. "What for?"

"We don't get along, we have nothing in common. We should separate for a few days and see what happens."

"No, it's a stupid idea. If we don't get along it's your fault. You never come with me to the country. You have nothing in your head but the piano."

"All right, let's try. Let's go together to your country place for the weekend."

He hesitated: "You want to go—" I knew the offer was upsetting, I was intruding, and I could sense his resentment. But it was my turn to pressure. "Yes, just you and I."

It was hard for him to pull out, so that weekend we left. The country house had a cold, damp, sad charm. Under a thin coat of forced politeness I felt he actually hated me. His property was very isolated and so quiet; I was at his mercy. I felt danger, as if he wanted to kill me. I shivered with fright. Why had I come?

I continued to try at marriage, however.

After several months my mother suggested "Why don't you go to the mountains? Drop everything and go rest for a fortnight. That will change your perspective and when you return you'll be in a much better condition." I thought she might be right.

Guy and Robert were both amateur skiers, and were delighted with my decision to go. The train rolled on toward Megève. Tired of pressures and internal turmoil, I shook off some of my anxieties. I knew Cortot was on a tour. Where was he? Also on a train? Was he working? What difference! He wasn't with me. I must have sighed.

"What's the matter?" Robert asked.

"Nothing."

"Does my presence put you in such a bad mood?" I said nothing, but my expression begged him for peace. "No scenes, please," I wanted to say, "I can't bear it." But he continued, "Is it such an effort not to see Cortot for a fortnight?"

"Oh, leave me alone." Rising, I went to lean out of the corridor window.

After dinner Guy said good night and whispered in my ear, "Come to my room, I want to talk to you."

I hurried to Guy's room. "What is it?"

"Sit down. Be calm and don't try to answer immediately." He chose his words as if he had to accomplish an annoying duty.

"No, I'd rather stand. Speak. What has happened?" Guy looked at me for a few moments. He watched me closely, as if to ascertain how I would react.

"Mother telephoned me just as we were leaving. She wanted me to tell you that Cortot plays on the tenth in Geneva. Bethsabée will stop one night in Geneva to hear him on her way home. Mother didn't want to keep it from you, but she begs you not to go." I leaned against the side of Guy's compartment. He kept on talking, but I no longer understood what he was saying. Suddenly Guy stopped. "What's the matter? What has come over you? Anyway, I've done my duty, and now do as you wish."

"Good night," I said and shut myself in my own compartment. I cared for my mother, I respected her and genuinely wanted to please her. "Mother begs me not to go," I thought. "But why did she ask that of me? She knows I can't keep away."

It was the tenth, and I joined Bethsabée in Geneva. Cortot opened with the twenty-four Chopin Preludes.

"He is tired," I murmured as I sat down. I breathed uneasily, fearing he would play less well. But I forgot all about fear when he played the Sonata in B-flat minor. Breathlessly, as in a dream, I followed the funeral procession as it slowly approached. This sonata, which I was hearing for the first time, was a complete revelation. After the concert Cortot looked puzzled at meeting me.

"What are you doing here?"

"I was in the mountains nearby and I couldn't resist the temptation to come and hear you."

"Are you going to Lausanne, by any chance? I play there tomorrow."

"I am going back to my mountain peak."

Was his question sarcastic? Did I deserve that irony? He said that this unexpected meeting had given him pleasure and excused himself for having to leave me quickly. He held out his hand with a slight smile, one of his most disarming smiles. Dismissed. Had I really hoped for more! I suppose that it is almost impossible to tell a woman that she doesn't attract you.

[25]

A Step Forward

Several months passed. I heard Cortot play in Cannes. He gave the same Chopin recital and played sublimely. Always amiable, charming, always distant, this time he refused my mother's invitation to dinner. He played the next day at Nice, but I had the courage not to go back after the concert to congratulate him. I contented myself with anonymously sending him carnations.

I didn't really think I would meet Cortot again, and my heart beat faster when in Paris I saw his car stop before the Salle Pleyel where one of his students, Ruth Slenczynska, a child prodigy, was giving a recital. We exchanged a few words and I sat down beside my mother. Cortot stood not far off. I could hear his voice, feel his presence, but I dared not turn around. He came forward a bit. He drew near and sat in the chair behind me. He leaned forward and put his arm on the back of my chair. I could feel the sleeve of his jacket. Little Ruth seemed to enjoy playing Chopin's Étude in Thirds. Then she played the Italian Concerto of Bach. The crowd applauded. What did it matter, their admiration, the noise, the excitement?

Ruth Slenczynska at seven years old was a powerful prodigy. She was short for her age, and stocky. These characteristics made her appear even younger; thus she struck her audience as a phenomenon. But I couldn't think of Ruth. Cortot was here, very near, and he was speaking to me.

"I must hear you again," he offered. "I've been so busy lately." My heart skipped a beat. Another chance when I least expected it!

For several years I had lived for him. Yet had I the right to impose obligations on him which he didn't want? I decided to make him hear the truth, show him my feelings, and await my fate. My mother was giving a reception to present little Ruth and I was helping. I planned to ask Cortot to sign his picture so I would be able to talk to him.

"Yes, willingly."

"What day?" I asked.

He was going to come and hear me play. "I haven't my appointment book with me. We will make a date next Wednesday at the lecture, if you will," he continued.

Besides the excitement of Cortot's coming visit, I also worried that Robert would find out, but days went by naturally enough and Cortot came to see me.

"Will you have a glass of port?"

"No, thank you, nothing." I offered him a cigarette and lit one of my own. He seemed cheerful and quite relaxed, which was unusual for him. We spoke more intimately. I wanted to tell him everything. Don't you know how much I love you? But the words wouldn't come. They stuck in my throat. I wanted to fall into his arms but I couldn't. Instead, I told him of my unhappy marriage.

"Why don't you have children? They would be a source of happiness."

"With a man I don't love?"

"Is there a reason not to love him?" My cigarette trembled in my fingers. I raised my eyes. It was Alfred Cortot sitting there, awaiting an answer.

"Does one know why one loves, or why one doesn't love? Because it is he—because it is she—" I smiled, trying to be coy, but I knew my charm did not flow naturally. Cortot, expecting me to continue, said nothing. "The reason for my marriage is difficult to justify." His look encouraged me to be more explicit. "A combination of circumstances pushed me to it." I hesitated slightly and lowered my voice. "I wanted to be free— to work—and I wanted to know you." I dared not face him as I made my confession. He remained silent. Astonished, I looked up with conviction. "It's true," I affirmed.

"You didn't need to get married for that," he finally said to avoid an embarrassing situation. Once more he had evaded me. He spoke to me in a friendly way. A mark of interest. I told myself: Don't ask for the impossible. If he cannot give me love, isn't his sympathy valuable? Reason told me to be happy, but it was impossible. I must speak to him openly and force him to answer. But he was gone, out of the house.

My husband and I were indifferent to each other and we had each developed our own routine. I had entered the École Normale and was practicing piano in preparation for a coming exam. But as I became stronger Robert became less secure. He tried speaking to me more, showed jealousy of Cortot almost as if he wanted to save our marriage. He also tried coming to bed with me, but blamed me for sexual incompatibility.

Following a performance at the École Normale a few days after I had spoken to Cortot, his car was not waiting for him. I immediately offered to drive him home. He refused. I tried to insist. "No, no," he said, and rushed off in a cab. I was stunned. I knew he was avoiding me because I had opened up a little to him. Guilt and shame crushed me, as I felt ugly and unwanted.

When I got home, I collapsed on the bed and tears filled my eyes. As Robert entered my room and sat on the edge of the bed, I tried to be friendly. "Where did you dine?" I asked in a toneless voice.

"At Hermenonville with Louis," he answered. I looked at him with a faint smile.

"You don't believe me?" he asked.

"I really don't care with whom you dine," I answered. He tightened his lips angrily and started pacing the floor. I lay quiet for a while, watching him go back and forth. Then I said, "I am very tired, I need sleep, good night."

"Is that all you can say to me, 'leave me, I need sleep'? You abandon me all evening and when I come in you greet me looking like death. What *is* the matter with you? Didn't Cortot smile the right way?" I didn't answer, as I was barely listening to him. I could only see Cortot leaving in a cab. After a long silence Robert screamed with anger, "You don't want to see me anymore? Say it, you don't want to see me—right?"

"Tonight I'm very tired. We will discuss this tomorrow when you have calmed down. If you don't let me sleep I will fail my exam and I'll get sick."

"I don't care a damn about your exam. It is imbecility. Just sleep in the morning." He put his fist on my chin. "You deserve a smashed face. I feel like punching your nose in." He clenched his teeth as if to control his mounting rage. I turned the light off by the bed. Suddenly the room became dark. He tried to put the light on, but I fought him. Out of control, he tore the wire from the wall, smashed the lamp on the floor, ran to the door and turned on the ceiling light. With flaring nostrils and bulging eyes he came back to me and shook me by the shoulders, screaming in my face. "You will not get the better of me. I will never let you get me, you and Cortot. Do you *hear* me? Answer me, do you hear me?"

Yes, I heard, but with indifference. "I never talk with furies," I said quietly. "If you really want, we will discuss it tomorrow." I thought for a moment that he was going to strangle me, but I didn't move. Suddenly he let go, got up and left the room, slamming the door.

I wanted a better life. He was hanging on. I told him I was going to my mother for a few days to relieve the tension and have a chance to think. That evening I took a nightgown and a toothbrush and went to my parents. I left Robert a note confirming what I had already told him and assuring him that a few days' separation could only be helpful to both of us.

Shortly after I reached my parents' house, while my mother was in her bed of crêpe de Chine sheets and satin covers and I was sitting in an armchair at the foot of her bed, there was a brief knock on the door. Without waiting to be invited in, Robert entered. "I want you to come home with me," he commanded from the door.

"No, I am going to stay here for a few days, then we'll see."

"You're coming home with me, now." His voice was low and stubborn. I knew he wouldn't listen to me. He was nervous, tense, driven by an inner compulsion to get me back. My mother kept silent as my discomfort grew. Robert stood in the middle of the room, staring into space: "You're coming home, you're coming home," he ordered, faster and faster. Still in the armchair, I answered as positively and as quietly as possible, "No, I am not."

He suddenly looked at me. "You're not?" and from his pocket he pulled a gun. Somewhat unsteady on his feet, he waved it around. A moment of fear: for a second I wondered whom he would shoot—my mother, or me, or both? Instead, he turned the gun toward his chest, pulled the trigger and fell onto the foot of the bed. I rushed over to him, took the gun which was still in his hand. I hid the gun in the next room while my frightened mother ran down the hall in her transparent night-gown, to the bewilderment of the footmen. Robert's older cousin was called to come and take care of him. The bullet hadn't touched him. Fortunately, it had gone through his jacket and landed in the wall behind him.

Of course, I never went back. Eventually I returned to the avenue Foch, this time really on my own.

[26]

Head On

After having taken a first step to improve my home life, I decided to confront Cortot head on by talking to him openly and forcing him to respond. But rather than really trying to reach Cortot, I was probably trying to find an outlet for my inner pressure.

The day arrived when Cortot came to me once more. Seated at my desk, he turned the leaves of a first edition of Schumann's "Les Études Symphoniques" that I had just acquired. As he silently examined each page I was nervous. "Don't be a coward," I said to myself. "It is now or never, say something to him now; in a moment it will be too late."

I was determined, so I began by making small talk. "Are you happy at the approach of the summer?"

Cortot answered easily enough, "The summer isn't beginning very well for me. I must go to Brides-les-Baines for my wife, and I have to play twice in August, which is hard for me, but I can't get out of it."

I wished to conceal my nervousness, but I spoke in a breathless voice, a voice not quite my own, a bit like an automaton, "Aren't you going on tour in October?"

"Yes," he replied. Abruptly I made my move: "Take me with you." At first he pretended not to hear. I repeated, "I am very serious. Take me along."

Cortot remained expressionless; then he gave a little laugh. "What about your mother?"

"My mother—I'll write to her."

"No, I mean, what will she think?"

"I don't care what she thinks."

"Oh!" he protested. "And what will the world say?"

"We needn't be slaves of the others."

"No, but—"

But what? I thought. What do these objections mean? A thousand excuses to avoid saying "I don't want you." I stiffened to hold back tears. Instead of begging and opening my heart I said only, "I won't disturb you." To put an end to it he said, "But you must see that I can't, I'm not free, I have the most tender feeling for my wife." I was ruined by these words.

"All is over," I thought. "He won't want to see me again. Isn't that what I really wanted, to rid myself of the past and the present?" Now I realize it was, but I couldn't understand that at the time. He was close to me and I wanted his arms around me, wanted to feel his lips. I stared at him, imploring him for a kind gesture, but he didn't see. He was looking fixedly at his knees. "Are you angry at me?" I asked.

Cortot didn't answer immediately. Each of his words was measured, each of his thoughts willed, each of his gestures controlled. For several moments he searched for the right word. "How could I be angry?" He squeezed my hand gently. It was too late. Why didn't he have even the slightest spontaneous response?

"I am not saying this so much on my account, but—" he made a vague gesture with his hand without finishing the sentence. "Once or twice in my life I met a younger person who was able to bring me something my wife couldn't. But that was different—" Those words cut me with a sharp pain. Sensing it, he continued, "One can never say what one would like to. It's difficult to fight oneself." A few seconds went by, then he said, "Now I must leave. I have a lecture to prepare."

"So soon?" my exclamation escaped. Cortot waited a moment. "Have courage," he offered. Without answering, I made a vague gesture of abandonment. He hesitated, as if he wanted to say more, but restrained himself.

That evening I still went to his lecture and appeared calm in his presence. But I wasn't really that upset. I had made a giant step forward to make my dreams a reality, to not live in a fantasy world of passions but in a self-constructed world, far away and beyond Miss Swainston or my parents. I was attempting to grow up. In a way, Cortot was a tool, a crutch, to help me develop my own person. If it hadn't been Cortot it probably would have been another great artist.

Having told him outright how I felt was a tremendous relief. And though my interest in him continued, it became less tense while remaining deeply part of my dream to achieve, to work, to get somewhere on my own merit. In fact, practice and music filled my life and kept me from feeling sorry for myself. But meetings with Cortot were still very important. He made no allusion to my confession, and I was grateful for that. We became friends, in a way, as he spoke to me about life—once he said: "The ideal consists of doing good where needed, of helping others. You reach others by developing yourself." I began to reason that it was not Cortot I loved, but myself. He had awakened me in a thousand unsuspected ways. Then I recalled an evening after a private concert when I had given him a facsimile of a Liszt manuscript. He'd thanked me and had taken my hands in his. "How kind," he'd said. I'd been excited by his touch. Wasn't this love? I wanted to think that I still loved him, although by now I was well aware that I had begun to free myself from this obsession. I made an attempt to be social. I met a friend for dinner. In the course of the meal the woman began to speak of Jacques Thibaud. "I hear he is terrible with women," I said casually. "It seems, however, that he is successful."

"Oh, he isn't the only one; Alfred Cortot also. A friend of Thibaud's told me that."

My friend was astonished that I didn't bombard her with questions. I fell silent as she proceeded to talk. "His mistress is Egyptian, a short brunette, a pronounced type, very intelligent, they say. But she is tubercular."

I burst out, "I am bored with idle gossip. Is there nothing more interesting?" My friend gasped, swearing that all she had wanted to do was to entertain me. But it was the final stroke. There it was: Cortot loved another, and not his wife.

Back home I looked at his portrait, at his fakir's eyes, with mounting resentment. I remembered a sentence I had scarcely noticed when he'd first said it: "One is never completely safe no matter how careful one may be." He might have been trying to tell me about his mistress, but I'd been thinking of myself rather than listening to him.

Looking back now, I realize I was more interested in unloading myself rather than reaching Cortot. Struggling through a very rough adolescence, part of me didn't really want him to accept my love. Because of my ambivalent feeling toward Cortot, I may have had my car accident on my way to visit him the previous summer.

And in time as I aspired to real love I was able to develop a more normal friendship with him, and eventually to accept his Egyptian mistress. I became friendly with both of them, and I even accompanied them on a couple of small concert tours.

III

Success

[27]

Meeting Grisha

Shortly after Robert's shooting, I moved out of my parents' home to what had been my aunt's house—a large property on avenue Foch. Besides the bedrooms there were several salons, a ballroom which I never furnished, and a very large dining room. One of the salons opened on a stone terrace and down a few steps into a lovely large garden. Though this was like a little palace, it was very small compared to the rue St. Florentin where I had been raised. A very spacious bathroom in which I felt comfortable adjoined my bedroom. Preferring its informality to the pompousness of a drawing room where my mother would have settled, I sat at its dressing table to read and to write so in a way I used it as a sitting room. I lived between the piano and the bathroom.

As the divorce process came to an end, I was a free woman living alone. I could do anything I wanted. No need to report to any authority, no restrictions. But my only interest was practicing piano. Cortot's picture was still with me. What had become of all my dreams, passions, and despair? Where was the boiling tornado that used to gnaw at my insides? Days and weeks went by, monotonous and lonely. I now wished I could meet someone nice, someone who would really care for me, someone I could love. But in my withdrawn castle, sheltered and self-restricted, there was little chance of success. "I will never find anyone," I murmured. "No, I will never get married again because dishonest men will be after my money and the honest man will shy away from too much money. It is hopeless." Filled with sadness, I returned to the piano. I had practiced enough so I could play a couple of pieces, but music didn't come naturally to me.

At the time when monotony seemed to dull my future, my parents gave a party at which a woman entertained the guests by reading the future in the palms of their hands. I put out my hand. She looked for quite a while, then said, somewhat reluctantly, "I see success—yes, success—but not in your present occupation."

"Not with my piano?" I said, somewhat disappointed.

"No, not with anything you have today, but I see success." That left me bewildered. At the time I was convinced her prediction was absurd, but it felt good.

Then one day a pianist friend of my parents, Ania Dorfmann, came to me and said, "I have a friend I think you should meet. He is a Russian cellist, giving a recital next week. Why don't you come and hear him with me?" I went, but I mustn't have been very impressed as nothing of that evening remained in my memory. In fact, I cannot even remember having gone to that concert. However, soon after, I met the cellist, Gregor Piatigorsky, at a very small gathering at Ania Dorfmann's apartment. In social gatherings I was shy and awkward. Having grown up alone, I was totally inexperienced in superficial conversation. I never knew what to say, so I remained silent. I sensed that meeting Grisha was perhaps the opening to a potential date, but I was lost in my own dreams; and though I was hoping to find a husband, I was not really ready to reach out. Of course, after my involvement with Cortot who was so famous, I wasn't impressed by a known cellist. I looked only for a human being to love and who would love me.

I didn't expect to have any success with men. So lonely, I went back to practicing piano and I told the concierge not to disturb me (all telephone calls were received centrally by the concierge). And when Gregor Piatigorsky called, he was told that I could not be disturbed. But when I realized I had missed his call I was very upset. Though I hoped he would call again I

didn't really expect him to, so I was surprised and happy when
he did.

"I would like to see you again," he said on the phone,
"maybe we could go out—"

"Yes, I would like to."

"When can I see you?"

"Do you play golf?" I ventured.

"Yes . . . yes, I do."

"Then let's play Friday." I had a date! And I was happy.

Grisha had never been on a golf course. In brand-new shoes
he had bought for the occasion (which unfortunately were too
small) he fumbled the ball. Years later he told me how much
he had suffered on that first date, as each step was painful. And
in spite of sore feet and my offending suggestion that he improve his golf, he wanted to join me for the summer!

When I told my mother she warned, "Be careful."

"What do you mean?" I asked. "He's very nice."

"But you don't know him."

I wanted Grisha to drive down with me to Meautry so he
could see the horses with their fillies, but I was still insecure.
The disaster of my first marriage was not yet erased. Though I
was annoyed at my mother for creating doubts in me, I
thought she was right. I had encouraged a stranger. My old
fears rushed back. How will I manage? I wondered. Will I
know what to say? I looked at my mother and said, "I told him
he could come." She sensed my worries.

"You are going too fast," she said. "Don't do it."

"But we already agreed; I can't get out of it."

"It's easy," my mother said. "Just write and tell him your
plans have changed."

Unhappy and yet partly relieved, I composed a letter telling
Grisha that something had come up and I wasn't sure which
day I could leave, but that maybe I could still see him in Meautry. Grisha never answered my letter. I had defeated myself,
killed what I wanted most. And I spent a lonely summer.

When I returned to Paris, I was hoping to hear from him. I
waited for the mail, but there was never even a postcard. A
year went by and I knew I had lost my chance. I spent desperate hours at the piano, but I practiced inefficiently and without

aim. My chess board was always with me, almost as security. I ate most meals alone and was served by a footman as I had been in childhood. I went daily to my psychoanalyst. There was nothing to look forward to. I had dropped back into an empty routine. But I was lucky to still have Renée Ovise with me because in her silent way she was a support.

Partly to encourage me to be more social, my mother suggested that I help young musicians by inviting a few people to hear them. That seemed like a good idea. They would make a little money and get some exposure. So I arranged a few evenings that I called the Davidsbundler. Before the second such party Ania Dorfmann called to tell me that Gregor Piatigorsky was in town and asked if she might invite him.

"By all means, bring him along," I said. After all, I would see him again. That was exciting.

But he was still very angry at me for giving him the brush-off, so he refused and went straight to bed. I was disappointed when Ania Dorfmann arrived alone. Later he told me that something in him couldn't stay away. He got up, dressed on an impulse, and came. When he entered with a warm smile a half hour later, my heart skipped a beat. He stayed until everyone had gone. Later, when I told my brother that I had met someone very nice, he asked, "The tall English guy who stayed till the end?" I told him Grisha was not English, but Russian.

The following week Grisha came back a few times to rehearse with his accompanist, Ivor Newton. A year had passed and I was less scared, more ready to plunge into life, to accept reality. I was hungry for a happy exchange. I felt I could open the vault and defy the past.

After four and a half years of treatment, my involvement in psychoanalysis was coming to an end. It was time to stop, but I was lingering. On the piano next to the photo Grisha had given me of himself, Cortot's picture still stood. At twenty-four, on the verge of entering a new life, I was still hanging on to the past. It seemed difficult to face a total break. Grisha and I had been close for only a few weeks. Somehow my daily hour at the psychiatrist's created a wedge between us.

"We could go out tomorrow afternoon."

"No, I can't. I have to be at Dr. Loewenstein's at three o'clock."

"You don't need him anymore. It's ridiculous. When are you going to get out of that?" He was annoyed. Pointing to Cortot's picture, he added, "And get rid of that ugly face."

"I don't want to."

He picked up his own photo, tore it up. "Then you don't need me." He reached for his coat and hat.

"Where are you going?" I was distressed. He didn't answer. He just walked out.

Gone, without a word. I was in shock, left to stare at the closed door. For a while I stood stunned, then I took Cortot's picture and dumped it in a drawer. I wanted to run after Grisha, tell him only he counted. Get him back. Call out. Explain. But to no avail; he was gone, was unreachable. He had vanished. I waited for some time, crushed. No way to repair, to make good again.

I went to talk to Renée Ovise, my maid from childhood, whom I trusted.

"We had a fight. He's gone." She grunted something which meant "He'll come back." But an hour went by, then another. The shock and fear of losing him knocked sense into me and became the guillotine to my past.

The following weekend I went alone with my parents to Ferrières in the country, and fear returned. Would Grisha call back? I wondered. I sat on edge and waited. I jumped at each unusual sound and looked at the silent telephone until, finally, he called.

"When can I see you?" he asked. The concert season had just finished and he was ready to leave for the summer. "I can wait in Paris for a while if I can see you," he continued.

"Take a car, come here," I suggested. "It is only forty minutes from where you are."

He came and spent the following day in Ferrières with me. We walked in the park and he kissed me. Though I had been married over four years, this was really my very first kiss. Even though I hardly knew him, there was an understanding between us, a tenderness that went far beyond pure physical attraction.

Grisha was staying in a little hotel in the suburbs of Paris. He had no roots in any city. He had admirers and a number of casual friends, but in traveling from concert to concert he lived out of a suitcase and was very lonely. I invited him for dinner in Paris. It was a warm spring evening. The table was set out on the porch and we ate with the dim flickering light of candles.

On the stage Grisha was strong, imposing, and held his audience in suspense; in a social gathering he was entertaining, witty, and kept his audience laughing. But that evening he was quiet, a little overwhelmed, a little shy, almost like an overgrown lost child. We didn't have to speak much to feel close, to understand each other. Because he didn't force unnecessary conversation the evening was beautiful and emotionally filled. It was a dream, a fairy tale, and it was real. We spent several long evenings together before his next departure.

Then he had to go to London and Norway for concerts. There was no doubt in our minds that we belonged together, so I went with him. We crossed the Channel by night and I slept, or rather tried to, on a very narrow board that might have been called a bed. After the concerts we went up through the fjords. At one place the water looked very tempting. For so many years the ocean had been forbidden; my craving for it was still alive and part of me wanted to show off, so I jumped into icy cold water and found myself surrounded by jellyfish. I got out faster than I had jumped in. Long afterward, Grisha laughed at me for jumping into jellyfish.

Later, back in Ferrières, Grisha listened to me play, then put an easy piece of music in front of me and asked me to accompany him. I looked at him. "I can't," I told him.

"Try anyhow," he said, and sat with his cello, waiting to play. I tried, I fumbled and stuttered on the piano. "Your rhythm," he said. "Count one, two, three, four." I couldn't sight-read, I couldn't keep time. I had practiced endless hours. The piano had been the entire focus of my drive to break out of three worlds which imprisoned me—my childhood with Nanny, my parents' world, and my inner thundering world of despair. Several years of effort were crumbling to nothing. I was falling into a dark abyss.

"Your teacher is criminal," he finally said as I sat very silently, my arms hanging. But I knew it wasn't my teacher's fault if I wasn't capable. "She kept leading you on but never taught you music." He was appalled. But he was so deeply kind and enormously sensitive. He understood that I was crushed.

"Come on, let's go for a walk," he said, and we went in the park under the chestnut trees past the deer, down by the lake. I took his arm and closed my hand in his in total abandon. We were not talking but we were so close. He put his other hand over mine and with melting eyes and an immense tenderness whispered, "Ptichka—Kak ptichka—like a little bird."

I stopped practicing piano but that was no solution, so Grisha came to me one day with a bassoon he had bought for me. He said, "This is better suited for you than piano. It is the same register as the cello. There are less notes to play so there is no need to play as fast."

Before departing for the summer on a concert tour around the world he left me with my new toy. He was scheduled to play in Ceylon, Madagascar, and the Dutch Indies, coming back through Hawaii and San Francisco. We had become very close so I was to meet him in Hawaii to be with him on his tour in the United States.

But before leaving he wanted to share his happiness with his two best friends, Horowitz and Milstein, so we invited them to spend a day in Ferrières. I got a gift for each of them and carefully planned their favorite food. We got dressed and waited with great anticipation. It was almost time for their arrival when the phone rang and Horowitz canceled. It was disappointing, but we still looked forward to Milstein. A few minutes later, Milstein canceled. Grisha was stunned, angry and humiliated.

Until the age of eighteen I had never been alone in the street or in a store, and even after that I was driven everywhere by a private chauffeur. I had never been in a market or even seen the kitchen. I had never dialed a phone, made a call myself or even seen a public phone. And now I was planning to cross the ocean on a boat to New York, take a train to San Francisco and another ocean liner to Hawaii!

This was in the thirties, before air transportation. I was finally saying good-bye to the past, but leaving safety. I was de-fying every tradition of the time, violating every standard my parents stood for, and I was afraid.

What I had decided to do seemed impossible. And yet every-thing *was* possible.

Suddenly I received an anonymous letter threatening dan-ger. It said, "You are not crazy enough to run after that adven-turer, are you?" I read it with a heavy feeling in the pit of my stomach, showed it to Renée Ovise, my childhood maid and friend, and threw it away. "Dirt," she said, "disgusting." Her indignation had made her more eloquent than usual. Still afraid to leave alone, I called an early childhood friend. "How would you like to come to the United States with me? I invite you."

"Do you mean it? It would be great!" There was nothing con-ventional about my friend, and with her Bohemian nature she was ready to leave on the spur of the moment.

And we left. I was so full of anxiety and fear that I spent the entire crossing in the cabin, sick with headaches and throwing up. When we reached New York my friend was bubbling. "Look, it is exciting, let's go out, come on."

I was exhausted, lost and frightened.

"You go, I'll wait for you," I said. I stayed in the hotel room, lonely, ashamed, and miserable. We spent the next three days on a train going to Los Angeles, only to discover when we fi-nally got there that the boats were on strike. So I couldn't go to Hawaii, and we waited two weeks and went to meet Grisha on his arrival in San Francisco, at which time my friend went home to her family.

28

Our First Few Years

There were concerts almost every night in a different city, and I was traveling with Grisha and his Russian accompanist, Pavlovsky. Between us love was infinite. Sometimes two people, who are in many respects different, just fit together; against all logic, their personalities interlock. Between us there could be no hesitation, no discussion; we were destined for each other. The question was not "Will you marry me?" or even "Shall we get married?" but "How will we squeeze a marriage between two concerts?" Well, we managed to do it!

After each concert someone gives a party for the artist, and after Grisha played at the University of Michigan in Ann Arbor, Mr. and Mrs. Sink, the local managers, gave the traditional party. I signed Jacqueline de Rothschild in their guest book. The next morning we got married in a private civil ceremony in Mr. Sink's home. Thus, on the same page in the guest book I was proud to sign "Jacqueline Piatigorsky." We had a glass of champagne and immediately left for a different town, another concert.

I got pregnant, to my great joy, but with so much traveling and carrying heavy suitcases I started to bleed in a railroad station in Tallahassee, Florida, where we were waiting for a connection. I knew fear and despair, and there was no time to consult a doctor. We were heading north with forty-eight hours of traveling by train ahead of us, so I got on the berth and didn't set foot on the floor until we reached our destination. By then the bleeding had stopped. I could barely believe my luck.

A few months later, when we got back to France, my parents arranged a small party for a religious ceremony.

In October, my daughter was born in Paris. She was the most beautiful baby in the world, big and powerful, weighing over eleven pounds. In 1937 in France they kept mothers in the hospital for three weeks. I guess she didn't like it any more than I did, as she screamed and screamed. Twenty-four hours after her birth Grisha had to leave for concerts. And I developed a fever, perhaps a reaction to his departure.

I soon discovered that life with a concertizing artist was not going to be easy. After I had nursed my daughter for three months, Grisha had to leave for a three-month concert tour in the United States. I knew it was impossible to drag a three-month-old baby on a concert tour so it became a choice: my baby or my husband. How could I leave either of them? I tried to reason. I thought: A baby will not miss me; he needs me more. So I got a French nurse and left my baby in my mother's home. That was the most painful decision I ever made.

A year and a half later the world was tense and dangerous. Jews were sent to concentration camps to be destroyed. As I needed someone to help me with the baby, rather than engage a local woman, I helped a Jewish person escape the Nazis. We called an agency. From a great number of applications it was a difficult choice, but we finally decided on a trained nurse working in a hospital in Vienna. She spoke French fluently, was knowledgeable and very kind. Kathe Kollman stayed with us for many years, and after she retired we still remained friends. At the time, it took several months for her papers to come through. They finally came as Grisha was leaving for his concert tour in the United States. This time I took my daughter and we settled in the Pierre Hotel in New York while her father was concertizing. In March, 1939, Mussolini had come under Hitler's influence. Austria had been annexed. War was imminent. Grisha had a Nansen passport which really was a certificate of identity issued by the French police and meant no nationality, no government protection, no working permit. It meant he would be instantly sent to the front lines to be killed as a simple soldier, and this even though he was thirty-six years old and a world-famous cellist.

In Chantilly, where we were for a short visit before the departure to the United States, the sun was out, insects were peacefully buzzing on the flowers, and Jephta, our daughter, was seventeen months old. Peace in the garden, heavy tension in the world. When, on March 15, 1939, Hitler entered Prague, Grisha panicked, overcome by uncontrollable fear that told him to run, get out in time, leave—just leave. Logic and control vanished. Driven amok by his raging fear, he said goodbye, took a suitcase, and left.

He had run away from the revolution in Russia, run away from Germany under Hitler, and now was running away from France. But when he got on the ship in Le Havre he remembered Jephta and me. It was only a few days before we had planned to leave together for the concert tour. Of course, he thought we would join him in less than a week. Suddenly a new fear besieged him: we might be cut off and separated indefinitely. So, just as impetuously as he had left, he ran off the ship straight back to us, forgetting his suitcase on the boat! It had been frightening and sad to see him leave. But fear is contagious; and though I didn't feel the immediate danger, I wanted him to be safe.

I was sitting in bed in the early morning when he arrived. No warning. He just walked in, embarrassed, ashamed, but happy. He fell into my arms and, being together, we both felt protected. Eventually we left together on schedule for the concert tour in the United States.

As the tour came to an end, Grisha was tired; there always is a letdown at the end of a season. We were ready and looking forward to flying back to France for the summer. An acquaintance came and, full of enthusiasm, said, "I have something for you." Grisha looked at him and waited. "It's the most beautiful place; there are five hundred acres, a river, a house completely furnished. The government is selling it for very little because the taxes were not paid." He went on raving about this property in Elizabethtown, New York, in the heart of the Adirondacks. Grisha had foresight: a foothold in the United States sounded like a good idea. It might be important some day to have property in the United States, so he decided to drive up and see it. The first thing he noticed was birch trees, like those at home in Russia. He fell in love with those trees, with the rocks, the wilderness, and on an impulse offered five thousand dollars, knowing that for such a beautiful property that sum was ridiculous—almost a joke.

When we had left France two and a half months earlier we were escaping the oncoming war and feared we would not be able to return. But from a distance the dangers seemed less imminent. We almost forgot that in Europe the atmosphere was tense; people were on edge, loaded down with anxiety. Grisha had overcome his crisis of fear and now refused to believe in a war, so in June we left for France and forgot all about his bid for Windy Cliff.

We were spending the summer on Lake d'Annecy. Vacationing on the lake was beautiful. Rowing and hiking in the mountains were peaceful enough to make us forget the increasing tension and dangers of the outside world, though those dangers were mounting. Hitler kept invading; Chamberlain in London was making peaceful speeches. I was deeply involved with my baby and didn't follow the events closely, but Grisha was reading every news item and listening to the radio. So through him I knew more or less what was going on. He was worried but didn't really believe that war was imminent.

Unexpectedly a telegram arrived: "Congratulations, you bought the property!" Just as suddenly, one morning, without any apparent reason, I woke up worried. Maybe I realized what Hitler's August 23 pact of nonaggression with Russia entailed. In any case, on September first when he marched into Poland it became my turn to panic. I ran to Grisha: "We have to leave, we must leave right now."

"You're crazy. What is the rush?"

"We have to go, we are going *now*."

He looked at me, surprised. The intensity of my decision was like an avalanche nothing could hold back. But for a moment Grisha tried. "Jephta is out in the woods with Kathe," he said.

"Go and get her now, there is no time." My fear was contagious. He went out and brought Jephta back. In the meantime I called Paris to get room on a boat. Within the hour we packed a suitcase, took our two-year-old daughter, Kathe Kollman, the cello, the bassoon, and drove straight to Le Havre. We were lucky to get accommodations on the *Paris* as everything was already sold out. We got on the ship on the morning of September third, and two hours later France declared war.

The ship was frozen. No one was allowed on or off as we stood in the harbor. September 3, 1939 was a hot and muggy day. People were crowding the deck, walking aimlessly back and forth. The heat increased and breathing became hard as we waited. For two days and two nights we stayed in the harbor, full of anxiety, silent, hoping for news that did not come. Then suddenly the ship was released and we sailed. The crossing was rough as we went up and down with the swelling of each wave. I was pregnant again and my daughter was twenty-three months old, getting into everything, crawling on the deck because it was too rough for her to stand and run. I was so anxious to protect her that I forgot to be sick as I had always been in the past. Then I realized how much can be done if the need is deep enough.

As we arrived in the United States, Grisha and I looked at each other. We had a home in the Adirondacks! We came with nothing and went straight to Elizabethtown, New York, to get acquainted with it.

During the war, while the Germans were entering Paris from the north my parents escaped from the south and eventually flew to the United States. Grisha was particularly proud to offer them our home upon their arrival. Though we were happy to help them, their visits were never easy. In my childhood my mother had not established the proper relationship with me and, having been served all her life, she was demanding. Though she meant well and basically would have liked not to disturb, she didn't know how to be independent. She expected a lot from her surroundings.

If I had been stifled, even crippled in my youth, it didn't show in my ability to accept responsibilities in Elizabethtown, or to make decisions and raise a happy family. But in spite of that, I still felt insecure. I could not reach out and develop a

social life. Among people I seemed to be an outcast, and the
need to express myself and accomplish an activity of my own
was still gnawing at me. Our new home was actually a summer
resort, a lovely charming house at the top of a hill. Behind it
the mountain, heavily wooded and alive with animals, went up
for acres. In the winter the temperature reached 40 degrees
below zero, which would freeze the water pipes which were
above the ground. We were three miles from the closest village
of twelve hundred inhabitants which had no movie house and
no real hospital, but only a community house and one country
doctor. At the foot of the hill an abandoned caretaker's house
stood, and across the only road in the woods the Bouquet River
ran on a very rocky terrain. The river had deep spots for swimming and was fed by ice-cold little springs bubbling out of the
earth. Often when we went swimming we were visited by a
mother pig bringing her little ones down the river, and we all
swam together. Weeks later we met the pigs' owner, Mr. Otis, a
farmer who was our nearest neighbor. In contrast to my own
childhood when the farmer's children had silently stared at
me, Jephta and later Joram played with Mr. Otis's son, a very
nice quiet boy with a large smile.

As we couldn't stay in Windy Cliff when the weather got
cold, we rented a house in the village almost across from the
community house, where my son was born a few months later.
On the morning of his birth I was out on the skating rink with
Grisha and my daughter. From a distance we saw Dr. Gerson,
the only doctor within miles, and when the contractions
started we waved to him. Shortly after, the contractions increased and I entered the community house. The nurse put in a
call for Dr. Gerson. Though she did reach him, he decided that
he had plenty of time because he had just seen me on the skating rink, so he didn't come. The nurse kept calling him fran-
tically but could no longer locate him. Within a half hour she
was pushing the baby's head back. Dr. Gerson finally showed
up, and the baby was allowed out. My son, Joram, didn't come
into the world with a scream, but with a terrible silence for a
few seconds. Dr. Gerson held him by his feet, gently slapped
him on the back and, just as I was asking, "Is he alive?" life
came with a cry. Compared to my daughter, he was small. He

was born during the nurse's lunch hour so, without washing him, they wrapped him in a blanket and handed him to me. I took one look and said, "He is great!" but his father saw a dribbling, slimy mess and said, "How can you say 'He is great'?" We were alone, uprooted in a foreign country. But I had a son. Naturally, to me he was great.

After the first winter we remodeled the caretaker's house so we could remain at home when the weather got cold. We needed more help and we heard of an older couple who had escaped from the Nazis and were in desperate need of work, so we engaged them. They obviously had never done housework before. The man was a lovely gentleman who spent most of the time playing piano while his wife wrote poetry, and I ended up scrubbing floors.

I wore dungarees and a red hunting jacket and started smoking Grisha's cigars. I had two marvelous children, and we were lost in the wilderness. It was beautiful. One hardly knew there was a war raging in Europe. Unfortunately, however, life was not easy for Grisha, who went on long tiring concert tours and came home to undisciplined children, raccoons in the garbage cans, porcupines eating the fresh buds on the treetops and chewing the wood under the house, a butler playing a piano and a wife blowing into a bassoon, mostly out of tune.

Our household was anything but conventional. Grisha had been on a concert tour for several weeks and while he was gone I engaged an additional housekeeper: a black woman, tall, thin, reserved, and a little shy. Grisha came home while I was getting the children off to school. The new maid, not expecting him, was surprised to see a strange man walk in. Tentatively she went to him: "What can I do for you, sir?"

"Nothing, thank you, I am going to take a bath."

"A bath!" she answered incredulous.

"Yes," Grisha said without any explanation, and off he went with a smile to take his bath.

In spite of a full family life in Elizabethtown I still had the burning desire to do something myself.

I had a chart for the fingerings and, alone, had taught myself how to play the bassoon.

But my real love was chess. Chess was part of my blood. Of

course, in the winter there was no one to play with in Elizabethtown, so through a chess magazine I started to play by
correspondence, entering tournaments in which one played six
games at the same time. That was perfect for me. I had a small
pocket set which I always carried with me and I studied each
position in great depth. Before mailing out a move I was so
anxious not to make an error that even alone in the woods my
heart was beating hard. I went over each variation again and
again. I had to win.

29

Still Ambitious

Many interesting personalities—Charlie Poletti, Louis Untermeyer, Pauline Lord—filled Elizabethtown in the summers, but I was so preoccupied with my own surroundings that I was unable to see the outside world and I never met them. I don't even remember meeting the famous painter Wayman Adams who one summer made a very large portrait of Grisha playing cello, which won the Carnegie Award and now hangs at the Butler Institute of American Art in Columbus, Ohio. One of the great violin teachers, Ivan Galamian, had a summer school with very talented students.

The violinist Louis Persinger also had a summer home in Elizabethtown; he was a very good chess player, so naturally we played. I kept moving the pieces on the board when I analyzed positions by myself: I tried a variation, put the pieces back and restudied all possibilities, but in a regular game that isn't possible. One has to visualize the different positions in one's head. I had no experience of playing across the board so I lost, and I kept losing each time I played him. I was back in childhood. My mother had said, "I wish I also had a daughter that could win!" I was a loser, and I was angry. Persinger gave me a book on openings, so for the first time I started to study the game.

Noticing how upset I was, Grisha tried to help. He used to say, "You will meet two kinds of people: those who push you down and those who push you up. Stay away from those who push you down." Besides being a great artist, he belonged to the rare group who push people up. He helped anyone who came to him. Contact with him made people grow. He felt my frustration, and without any preparation said to me one day, "Why don't you learn to fly a plane?" He picked the very thing I was most afraid of! Out of fear, my parents had never flown, so for me, learning to fly almost meant overcoming a family taboo; but it sounded adventurous and exciting.

From Elizabethtown we drove nine miles to a tiny airport and found a man willing to teach me, and I started lessons on a Piper Cub. The greatest thrill came when I soloed for the first time. I kept on flying around the airfield, increasing my hours of solo. One day I needed papers from Philadelphia, so I decided to leave with my teacher in the early morning, get the papers and come home for dinner. After takeoff he noticed that the radio was not working so we came down in Schenectady, but because of the war the repairmen refused to attend to a private plane. We went on to Philadelphia and while I went for the papers my teacher had the radio repaired. We got home late and Grisha, very nervous and extremely worried, was waiting at the airport. But in spite of his own anxieties he encouraged me to keep on flying because he believed that learning to fly would give me the confidence I needed. At the time I was so involved with myself that I didn't realize how much my activity cost him in tension and worries.

When my daughter was of an age to go to school we moved back to the city and I had to stop flying. We spent one year in Stamford, Connecticut. The place we rented had a garden that went down to Long Island Sound and my old dreams of reaching water came rushing back, so in November I took a dip in the Sound. It was so cold that I could only get in and out, but it felt good. Then Grisha got a teaching position at the Curtis Institute in Philadelphia. We rented a place in Haverford on the Main Line. My daughter entered the Friends' Select School in Philadelphia. We took the train every morning but there was no time to go home and be back to pick her up, so I rented a room in a hotel and waited with my bassoon. This was inconvenient, so the following year we moved to an apartment on

Rittenhouse Square, one flight down from the conductor Eugene Ormandy.

I wanted to resume flying but was told that my teacher from Elizabethtown had killed himself in the plane on which I had been learning. That crushed my incentive. I decided not to push my luck.

Though I had never had any lessons, I was playing the bassoon well enough by then to enter an amateur orchestra as second bassoonist. I played in that orchestra for two years and enjoyed being part of a group, but was frustrated at not playing well enough.

I continued to play chess and went to the club from time to time. Among the players I met a man who seemed to enjoy playing with me. As he was quite good, I invited him to the apartment. His business was selling whiskey, and he was rather crude. In chess one deals with a cross-section of people. I played with a gardener and I played with Marcel Duchamp and Prokofiev, but after a couple of games, my opponent, the whiskey dealer, looked at the pictures of Grisha and the children, who were both asleep in the next room, then at me, and with some surprise said, "But you are in love with your family."

"Oh yes, very much."

He never came back. Yes, I was deeply in love with my family: the children, Grisha. My life was full and very busy, but my frustration was still there: the past wasn't erased. I sat and wondered and said to myself, You never learned anything so make up for it. Get an education, go to school; it's not too late. I went to the University of Pennsylvania and Temple University and was told that I couldn't enter without a high school degree or the French baccalaureate. I was determined to learn so I bought the necessary books to study for a high school diploma, and in the evenings when the children were asleep I studied. When I opened the chemistry book I couldn't understand a single word, so I stayed two weeks on the first page and a half until I had figured out the meaning of each symbol. I studied alone for a year and decided to try the state board examination. We were all in Elizabethtown, where we spent every summer, when those examinations were given. So I left the family and went to Philadelphia. I arrived the night before the exams to find all transportation on strike. I got very nervous: How would I get there by eight A.M.? I wondered. I got up at five and started to hitchhike on an empty stomach, as no coffee shops opened that early. It was very hot and muggy. I walked, ran, dripped with perspiration, got a ride, then another, and finally reached the location where the exams were given. I was tired, hot, and nervous and had to have some breakfast. The streets were crowded with striking workers. I asked one of them where I could get a cup of coffee. He said, "There is nothing around here, but if you want to come up to my apartment I can give you a cup of coffee." Without thinking how dangerous it could be, I went up. His place was an incredible mess. Dirty clothes on the floor, dirty dishes piled up high in the kitchen. He handed me a cup and filled it with old warm coffee, no sugar, no milk. I think there was no food in the apartment. However repulsive were the surroundings and the drink, I was grateful and happy to have it. He wouldn't accept any money. I added my empty cup to the pile of dirty dishes, thanked him, and left. For weeks after, I felt guilty not to have washed those dishes and improved the condition of his kitchen.

That morning I passed the state board examinations and I had a high school diploma! So in the fall I went back to Temple University and proudly handed it over. "Now can I enter the university?" I asked.

"You are now eligible to take entrance examinations," the secretary told me. I didn't know what that entailed, but I was ready to try. When the date came I was determined to do well, so I read the questions very slowly and carefully. By the time I had digested them a voice said, "Your time is up. Go to Part Two." No one had told me that the test was based on speed. I started to rush, but I had missed the easy part. When the results came the secretary called me in and said, "Your level is low; you are borderline. I can let you in on probation, but I honestly don't think you will be able to follow." I remained silent. Then she asked, "Do you want to try?"

"Yes," I answered.

Thus I was entered in a university. I enrolled in a mathematics course and an English course. In the English class they gave a little placement test. I had spoken English all my life, but I had never formally learned how to read or write. I did it by instinct and that misled the teacher, who put me in a more advanced class. Every week we had to write a paper, one week on an assigned subject, the other on anything we wanted. That was great. I could start to get "garbage" out of my system.

When the papers were returned in class the teacher said, "I am going to read you one paper because it is alive and felt." To my enormous surprise and bewilderment, he read my story. But when I got it back it was covered from top to bottom with red corrections, and after the A the teacher had written, "I graded it on its creative spirit and not on its endless chaos of English misusage." Somehow that made me smile. But at the end of the course there were very few red corrections. As for mathematics, it was easy. In spite of measles which I had caught from my children, I finished at the head of the class.

30

Starting to Achieve

Chemistry was the next class I entered, but the laboratory work required many extra hours, and that conflicted with family life. When Grisha came home for a couple of days between concerts I didn't want to spend those hours in school, so I dropped out. That was an important setback. Of course I had to make a choice, and probably deciding to place my husband and children above my personal development was a wise decision. Nevertheless, at that time I felt like a failure because I was not able to keep up with the requirements necessary to get an education.

One evening when the children were asleep and Grisha was on tour, I sat alone in the living room of our apartment on Rittenhouse Square. I felt empty, ashamed that I had dropped out of school. What to do? I picked up a pencil, looked at a chair in the corner and wondered if I could draw that chair. I tried, and drew the corner, a table with the couch and the armchair. I had done it! I looked at my masterpiece, which had a certain charm, but which also had something wrong. I couldn't figure out what it was. I had never had a drawing lesson in my life. I tried again. Two or three hours went by and I was still trying to figure out what was wrong. After spending most of the night working on my picture it finally looked right but had become stiff and lost its charm. My daughter was taking lessons at that time so at her next lesson I showed my two drawings, the one I liked but which seemed wrong, and the stilted one that appeared right. Her teacher, Madeline Ewing, said, "In the first one you used Chinese perspective. Your lines in space open up instead of converging." I didn't know what she meant, but I soon found out. "Try something else," she urged. "Draw a ball. Set up a little still-life with a doll or something." I did, and I kept on showing her my work until one day I asked the maid to sit for me and I tried a portrait. I still have that first charcoal portrait.

I kept on drawing and painting. As I had struggled to get the first drawing right, I continued to struggle, but all my work was stiff. I couldn't loosen up enough to express myself. Painting had come to me on the rebound and I was still ashamed of myself as a quitter.

About that time my son was continuously sick. With every cold he developed an ear infection. He was in school one week and in bed three weeks. We spent one winter in Florida where he was fine, but the following winter he got sick again. "There is nothing more I can do for you," said the doctor. "Move to a better climate." So we were uprooted once again and moved to Los Angeles, where many of Grisha's friends such as Rubinstein, Heifetz, and Stravinsky lived.

I tried to continue painting and piled up a great number of bad canvases. When things seemed difficult, chess was always there. I started to solve the weekly problems from *The Los Angeles Times* and sent in the results. The chess editor then was Herman Steiner, who had been United States champion in 1948. At an auction Grisha and I were bidding for a garnet pin, and it turned out that our opponents were Herman and Selma Steiner. We started to talk, and Herman remembered that I had been solving the paper's chess problems. Then he took us to his home where he was running a chess club above the garage. "Sit down and play a game," he offered, and introduced me to a tall young man, a very heavy stutterer. I played and lost. As I got up from the table, Herman Steiner caught me by surprise when he said, "You have just played your first tournament game." Though my mind was far away from tournaments, I remained in this first one. I finished somewhere in the middle, but as I had a natural ability for combinations I won the brilliancy prize.

I started to study with Herman Steiner and spent many hours trying to improve my game. One day he told me that he had recommended that I be invited to play in the Women's U.S. Invitational National Championship. It was played in the Manhattan Chess Club in New York. Losing my first game was so traumatic that I wanted to thrash, beat, slash again, but there was nothing to slash. I had to be polite. So I left the club in Greenwich Village in the middle of the night and walked back alone to the Windsor Hotel on 58th Street. I didn't win the championship, but I held my own. So without realizing it I had become one of the ten best women players in the United States. But that did not mean enough to me: I hadn't won the tournament. I kept playing for the next three years.

In 1954, the first women's Chess Olympics was held in Emmen, Holland. United States Champion Gisella Gresser and I were the two representatives of our country. I was playing second board. There were twenty-six nations competing. Through a first tournament, we were divided into three groups. Mrs. Gresser and I landed in the second group, which we won, finishing eleventh. Mrs. Gresser left before the closing ceremony so I had to go up to receive the trophy. Everyone before me had made nice speeches, but when my turn came I was totally unprepared. I froze. Searching for something to say, I hesitated for a moment, a long, torturous moment; then, too afraid to say something wrong, I walked off the stage without a word.

After playing in the first Chess Olympics, I came back to a normal life. I was still participating in tournaments, though I hated the pressure. Competitive chess is tiring beyond belief. It is always played at night and, at that time, in a room full of smoke. An average tournament game lasts four hours. I was immensely nervous before starting. In a game, from the first move on, tension mounts and keeps accumulating with no outlet. Sometimes, out of exhaustion, it is easy to make a weak move or blunder a minute or two before the end of the game, throwing away four hours of concentrated effort. Chess is highly obsessional and compulsive, so after every game the rest of the night is spent going over variations. Sometimes the game is not finished in four hours. After adjournment, the position really needs studying; but if one stays up all night it is even harder to be alert the next day. Some players have a second to help them study the adjourned position. I kept saying, "I hate tournaments, I will give them up, but how can I give up, I have not won the U.S. title."

"If you win the U.S. you will want to go to the Interzonal and compete for the World Championship," my husband said.

"Oh, no," I answered. Somehow I was caught by surprise. It had never entered my head. Why hadn't I thought of it? Was it so different to be half a point behind the U.S. champion or be champion behind the world champion? Was it just a title that I was after, or was there a deeper meaning to my dreams? Suddenly, winning the U.S. championship seemed a little less important, but I wasn't ready to give up. A few years later, when my children were both away and Grisha was starting to age, I did quit tournament chess. I was still roaming around the world with a distorted perspective, crushed by meaningless losses or overelated by meaningless wins. I had played since I was six years old. Chess had an obsessional grip on me, chess was my friend, my support. Chess was a refuge from unfairness. It had become part of my blood. Still, today, when I am exhausted and sad, when hope disappears, my natural impulse is to flop in front of a chess board and start pushing pieces. Variations take form; rush forward, retreat, attack, defend— no, an error, try again. Interest and vitality reborn flow into combinations, soon become storms, a typhoon in a teacup. It is ironic that chess and its combinations which are so sterile also awake a passion, bring life. On the little board, pieces grow and shrink like birds in a muddy marsh.

In the meantime, the children were growing up, and so was I. Through them, and with them, I was reliving my childhood; this time a happy one. We went to the beach together and as I followed them into the ocean it was one of my greatest joys to be seized by the cold water, then to jump into the waves, crouch and let them crash over my head as they brought warmth. How wonderful! I seemed to be reborn.

The children and I dressed up every Saturday and went to the movies. We had so much fun together that we called ourselves The Three Musketeers. But in the pool, I was embarrassed not to swim as well as they did. When my son was very young he tried to teach me how to swim underwater. I couldn't really do it, so when everyone was asleep at night I went to the pool and practiced underwater swimming until, chilled, I developed bad cramps and quit nighttime practicing.

When my son was thirteen I talked him into trying tennis; his sister was already playing well. He was still too young to drive so we went together to Rustic Canyon public courts fifteen minutes away. I sat and watched him practice with a very short Rumanian teacher who made tennis fun for everyone around him. I had played a few times in my childhood, so after a few weeks I became restless and wanted also to try to hit the ball, but I was recovering from abdominal surgery. I was so weak at first that I stayed barely five minutes on the court, but it was fun. Little by little my strength returned and I found myself waiting and looking forward to the weekly hour. During my lesson, my son, who had an exceptional talent for the game, played with other boys and sometimes got into a doubles match with adults.

My lessons continued for several years, but with my competitive and compulsive nature tennis went beyond being only fun. I was starting to improve; I wanted to be good. I wanted to win.

My son became a very fine player and loved to play after school. At that time he was going to Black Fox Military School across the street from the Los Angeles Tennis Club. I applied to the club for him, thinking that it would be nice if he could play for an hour before coming home. But they refused to allow him in. An acquaintance told us that he was unacceptable because he was a Jew. So, I immediately built a court at home, and he became a better player than most of the boys of his generation.

My husband was happy when I played tennis. "It is good for you; it is so much more healthy than chess," he would say. "You are out in the fresh air with sun; that alone is winning. You are having fun; you can't lose."

Before my son became too good for me we used to practice together, and I felt so lucky to be able to play with him. The first tournament I won was a Mother-Son tournament in Coronado. I also played Mother-Daughter, but we didn't do as well.

31

Sharing with My Children

"How did you develop such a wonderful relationship with your children?" I have been asked many times.

"I don't know." I have always answered, "I grew up with them, I think."

From the minute Jephta and Joram were born I was crazy about them. Not unusual. Even when their time and interest is elsewhere, most mothers love their babies. Although they sometimes entrust their children to baby sitters or English nannies they still love them! To me Jephta and Joram were the greatest treasures on earth. Long before they could talk, they were my little friends. When I smiled, they, confident and unreserved, gave back big smiles. Their entire little bodies lit up with pleasure.

Sharing fun with one's children is important to a good relationship with them. Jephta, Joram, and I did have fun together. We ran, climbed rocks in Elizabethtown, swam in the ice-cold Bucket River. I had a little motorcycle with a side seat and they took turns riding with me the three miles to the market.

We shared fun equally because we always participated in activities we all enjoyed. It was never a duty for me to care for my children. I was selfishly with them for my own pleasure, even though I knew I also had to guide them. But most of all I knew they needed understanding.

When Joram was six we lived in Philadelphia. One morning as he dressed, he was irritable and instead of buckling his belt he burst into a tantrum. He did that several other mornings. At first I couldn't understand his reaction but I finally realized he wanted more independence. He was fighting to grow up. So during the next tantrum instead of expressing exasperation and anger, I said, "Would you like to go alone to the park today?"

He stopped fussing and looked at me, surprised.

"You're a big boy now. You will have only one difficult street to cross; if you are really careful you can go alone."

As he walked out of the apartment and took the elevator downstairs, I saw that he was proud although a little apprehensive. I stood in the living room window with my heart pounding and watched him cross into the square. He got across safely and the tantrums ended.

If I understood my children, they understood me in return. When I was disagreable after losing a chess game, they knew it wasn't dangerous. They said, "It doesn't matter, Mom. You'll win next time," or "Poor Mom's in a bad mood." They said to each other, "She lost a game, it'll pass."

I discovered teaching children cannot be achieved with reproaches but by praising their slightest effort. When Jephta and Joram didn't do their homework or learn a boring history lesson, rather than say, "You're lazy," I just sat down and did it with them and *I* learned often as much as they did, and as friends we shared the boredom as well as the fun.

Shortly after we had moved to Los Angeles, Jephta, who had just entered her teens, was invited to a beach party. I had heard that at beach parties young people drank and entered into loose sexual relationships, so I automatically said, "No, you can't go."

But Jephta was struggling with adolescence so when I refused to let her go she was very upset and very angry and I realized then that she craved the same freedom as her friends. I didn't want to curb her development. So the next morning I called several aquaintances to get more information about beach parties. I was told, yes in general they *were* very loose but this particular group Jephta wanted to go with was decent and safe, so I decided Jephta could go.

After this my children knew that I would never be negative out of unreasonable fear or stubbornness. So when I had to say "No," they understood and did not fight me. They felt no need to fight to assert themselves. There was no room for a battle of wills.

32

Rothschild but a Girl

Many books have been written about the Rothschilds: the bankers, their help in international politics and in wars, their philanthropy, their shrewdness in making money, their lavish social entertainments, their ability to work, their family pride, and their persecution as Jews.

The name Rothschild was derived from the sign *Schild* or *Shield* that marked the house of my great-great-grandfather, Mayer Amschel, in the ghetto of Frankfurt, Germany. He had ten children; half were girls. From the original family, only the five brothers from Frankfurt are ever mentioned. Of the five young men, the two powerful brains were Nathan, who went to England, and my great-grandfather, James, who settled in France. Of the remaining three, one stayed in Germany and the other two went to Italy and Vienna, but they were not successful. The brothers all remained in close contact, communicating the intricacies of business dealings to one another by handwritten, personally delivered letters written in Yiddish or Hebrew. Most of their correspondence remains untranslated in the Rothschild Archives in London.

As the men worked together the women were ignored. They were only interim Rothschilds and, since they were going to be Rothschilds for a very short while, they were excluded from all the business enterprises. They were not even given the courtesy of being informed of the activities of their father and brothers.

Yes, I was a Rothschild, but I was a woman, an outsider, an outcast. Money wasn't mentioned at home except when, for instance, my parents discovered that their cooks had been cheating them by buying food and charging their employers much more than they had paid for it.

I never knew how much money I had, or even if I *had* money of my own, but I did know that nothing material was out of reach because I never heard the sentence "It is too expensive."

Because money was never referred to when I was growing up, my sense of values became affected. Money was no incentive for me to work. I wasn't even aware that money was of great importance to most individuals, and living in such ignorance distorted my relations with people.

The first encounter I had with the power of money in human relations came when I realized that Robert Calmann-Levy, during the four and one-half years of our marriage, had spent a great part of my fortune on his mistress. When I lived alone after divorcing him I thought love was barred from me by money (luckily I was mistaken). I was convinced that a man would only look at me for my money. I went to Renée Ovise for support and as usual she only gave me a sad smile to show that she understood.

The importance of money in people's lives was revealed to my sister without drama by a simple, casual statement. Bethsabée, already adult, had a friend who mentioned that she didn't take a trip because it was too expensive. All at once, a whole new concept of life opened up to my sister.

Sol Hurok, Grisha's manager, became very annoyed when Grisha was writing his book *Cellist* because he played fewer concerts while he was writing. One day when Hurok was having lunch with us he turned to me and said reproachfully, "Of course he refuses concerts; he does not need money!" That thought had never entered my mind. Grisha played less because he was so engrossed in writing, but he missed the stage and his public. Wanting to play and shying away from it tore him apart and tormented him. I started to wonder if his torment could have been avoided if the tangible reward, money, had been needed to send his children to school.

Financial ignorance stayed with me for many years. When

the war broke out and we left for the United States, my father told me he had put ten thousand dollars for me in New York for our immediate needs. I didn't know whether that was a little or a lot. Grisha thought that was all I had. He didn't discuss it with me. He just worked hard and paid all the bills. Having grown up surrounded by everything and not knowing where it came from, I simply continued by force of inertia to accept his effort. It took me many years to awaken and, eventually, learn that I could draw a check on my own account.

My father liked Grisha and was very happy when we married. He felt I was protected, well provided for, and finally settled. Ironically, when Grisha returned from a concert tour my father always asked him, "Did you make money?" But talking about business and money to me was still taboo. Maybe my father thought I knew what I had in the bank, that it had penetrated by osmosis! No, it had not, and my first introduction to figures was by a friend, Peter Fleck, who began managing my affairs after I moved to New York. As years went by our friendship became very close. When I was anxious that I was spending too much, I would call Peter; he always reassured me and sent me financial reports. But I was so conditioned to ignorance that I managed to drown in the maze of stocks bought and sold. I couldn't understand the reports. He was probably surprised at my continued innocence. "My dear Jacqueline," he told me when I kept asking if I was overspending, "you have a *lot* of money. What are you worried about?"

My children's fate as well as my own was entirely in Peter Fleck's hands. I relied on him blindly and totally, and he took care of us in a remarkable way. He was not only a financial father but a wonderful friend—solid, understanding, always supportive, intelligent, and kind. His modesty, his wide-ranging mind went way beyond the business world. In 1947 Peter created the Amsterdam Overseas Corporation, a financing company combined with an investment company owned jointly by Pierson, Heldring & Pierson, the Lambert Bank in Brussels, Belgium, and the French Rothschilds. That combination of financing and investment had not existed in the United States. Peter, who was president of the company, ran it in a conservative way. It was rather small but healthy, solid and respected. Eventually, with my brother's encouragement, he sold the financing company and the investment company became New Court Securities Corporation. In 1978, Pierson, Heldring & Pierson withdrew and the corporation passed equally into the hands of the English and French Rothschilds.

As Peter got older and started to consider retirement, he had enough foresight to choose a young boy, John Birkelund, out of business school and to train him thoroughly. When Birkelund became president, Peter remained chairman. Now he is retired as honorary chairman. Peter was helpful to my development not only because he is an intelligent and competent business-man, but also because he has a philosophical and idealistic drive. He studied theology and even became an ordained Unitarian minister. In business the aim is to acquire as much as possible, often at the expense of others, whereas the aim of a student of art or religion is to help others, sometimes at one's own expense. It is unusual to find both qualities in the same person.

When Mitterrand nationalized the banks in France, the family was very happy to take over New Court Securities, change its name to Rothschild, Inc., and enlarge it.

While I was growing up, the importance of boys went beyond the general importance placed on men by the times of male supremacy. The Rothschild boys formed a tight-knit, very secretive group, hungry for success. The demands on the boys were high. They had to live up to their name, to their social standing, and to their many responsibilities. So in addition to all the business, they inherited the extra allotment allowed by the government. My sister and I were so conditioned to the supremacy of boys that we never thought of injustice when Guy was favored.

Of course this situation did not affect the first few years of my life. Though still very young, my brother escaped Miss Swainston's power, and during the school years I did not understand the immense pressure for Guy to learn and achieve high grades when my father merely smiled at my failures.

Many Rothschild girls married cousins or even uncles because the wife of a Rothschild enjoyed the importance of being a Rothschild more than did a woman with the family genes who married an outsider. The men also preferred marrying in the family so their fortunes would accumulate and the business would remain private and tightly closed. For example, my great-grandfather James married his niece (his brother's daughter) and my grandfather, Alphonse, married his first cousin's daughter.

The Rothschild men were filled with the knowledge of their superiority—not only economic, but the superiority of their thinking, of their taste for art, of their talents. Some members of the family really were gifted, while through inbreeding others were a little degenerate; but as boys, they were all Rothschilds. Rothschild, unlike Rockefeller, did not mean only money. The legendary name was surrounded by a mysterious aura of power and symbolized a dynasty from which women and girls were excluded.

[33]

Learning

Whㅔn I was growing up in France it was in Ferrières that birds in the *faisanderie* and on the lake became part of me. Ferrières was not only a castle surrounded by a magnificent park, but I learned to play golf there; I bicycled for endless hours in the woods; I fed the deer shiny chestnuts that they ate from my hand; and I enjoyed forbidden chocolate.

Outside the park a very large orchard gave us our own fresh fruit daily: pears, pink velvet peaches, strawberries, raspberries, grapes, gooseberries, red and white cherries (rich and sweet), all cared for with love and presented to our dining room table with reverence. One of the alleys in the orchard was lined with trees shaped so as to spell ROTHSCHILD, a surprising and amazing achievement. In a number of greenhouses a knowledgeable gardener grew orchids of all kinds, from the regular cattleyas to a large variety of hybrids of different shapes and different colors, all started in test tubes. The first sign of an orchid's life was a tiny green dot emerging from the earth. When larger, the plant was transplanted until it had grown enough to join the other orchids in a warm, humid greenhouse.

Besides the farm in Pont-Carré my parents owned a second farm near the château where butter was churned. The fresh milk from the cows stood in huge urns until the cream on the top was thick enough to be moved into a different container, where it stood and was removed again when it was thick enough to make butter. The butter came to our dining room table in perfect circles three inches in diameter, three-quarters of an inch thick, with the five-arrow family symbol stamped in the center and dated around the edge as proof of its daily freshness. The cream was almost too thick to pour. With a teaspoon my father would take almost a pot of the cream at a time for breakfast, never failing to show by his eagerness how delicious it was to him. There was no other cream in the world as fresh, as rich, as succulent as cream from Ferrières. I liked spooning it into my mouth with a bar of dark chocolate.

In Ferrières there was also a special enclosure called the *chantier* for working with wood: cutting logs, brushwood and expertly tying little bundles for kindling wood. Outside the park, across the street, was a very large place called the *roseraie*, used only for growing flowers and roses, and from there fresh flowers were brought to the house almost daily. There were also stables with riding horses for my sister and me.

A specialized crew ran each of these departments. Growing up, I was only a spectator, as in a public zoo. I had never tried to milk a cow. In Ferrières I had no idea how such perfect fruit was produced, or which orchids were successful hybrids and which failed. I never learned where the birds and the monkeys in the *faisanderie* came from. I did not know their habits or what they ate. I never went into any of the cages. I lived surrounded by a fascinating and beautiful life, and yet I was an outsider. Later I blamed my ignorance on a lack of curiosity, on a failure to respond, but I suppose I was too completely absorbed by internal emotional upheavals to get interested in the life around me; later I discovered that neither my sister nor my brother knew any more than I did.

However, when my father died, my brother Guy, who until then had not taken much interest in the breeding of racehorses, picked up the newspaper and said, "There must be something to these horses," and immediately took over his father's interest. It is unfortunate that Guy had to wait until his father died to be interested. Guy also became head of the Rothschild Bank, until Mitterrand nationalized it; now he is retired and lives in France. Something inhibiting in the way we were raised, something crushing isolated us. Faced with infinite possibilities we could not take, still we would have liked to learn.

Yes, I had learned to play golf and to ride, but I had also learned to kill. I was killing birds! My sister, too, was taught how to handle a gun. Once she shot a deer but didn't kill it, and the wounded deer cried like a baby. This was so painful to my sister that she never again picked up a gun.

During three months of fall, my father arranged hunting parties in Ferrières. The French aristocracy were the so-called friends invited to those parties. Ten or twelve couples drove in on Fridays, staying two days, until Sunday night.

My father bred and raised pheasants, and while the woods were alive with those beautiful birds, the men settled in a row with guns. Guards surrounded the woods, beating and screaming so that the birds flew over the "heroic" hunters standing and waiting for them. The guns went off, the birds fell. The men were proud of their skill; they killed with smiles of satisfaction. The birds were picked up by the guards and by trained dogs, and were lined up on the ground so that the men could admire their slaughter. I looked at the long tails, the beautiful, colorful feathers.

I was fourteen when *I* was taught to kill. When I first became part of the hunting parties, I was proud to be the only woman included. To me the birds were only a target, but when they fell my heart sank before the massacre. I had become part of the men's brutality.

Yes, I killed, but part of me was also killed. Part of me was lying on the ground with the dead birds, their heads lined up, hanging lifelessly with open eyes. The peace of old cedar trees, the damp mystery of the woods, silent and alive, the dark soft humid atmosphere, the dim beauty and nostalgic sadness were crushed by death. The hunters repeated the round of killing four or five times during the day, until the time came to go in for afternoon tea. The women joined the men around a very large table. Besides a variety of cakes, they particularly savored hot chocolate and roasted chestnuts.

Why did I learn to kill instead of learning how to grow flowers? Though I loved nature, Ferrières sometimes became an enclosure from Kafka, which goes and goes and gets nowhere. The beautiful chestnut trees, the moss-covered earth and stone alleys, dark, soft, humid, seemed to have no end, no purpose. Dim beauty, sadness, a bicycle gliding forward to nowhere, a workman in denim overalls, a silent crossing of two worlds heading in opposite directions to reach emptiness—life moved in stillness, in a silent murmur, in peace, in death.

[34]

Stone Chooses Me

After I married Grisha and had children I had a full and happy life, but I was *still* trying to paint. Why? I'm not sure where the incentive came from. *Did* I still have childhood torments to eliminate? Or was I trying to live up to my environment? At rehearsals, musicians of all levels are alive with hope and enthusiasm, youngsters and students burst with ambition. I had tagged along, incapable of doing anything. It was both inspiring and oppressing. I was convinced I could never equal those around me, but in spite of my hopelessness something in me kept trying.

One day Grisha said, "Shirley Brody from the Young Musicians Foundation is coming to see me. She sculpts. You should meet her."

So I did. She took me to the San Fernando Valley to buy stones to work on. I picked a couple of small white ones called sugar stone, though they are very hard. We came home and Shirley Brody tried to show me how to cut them with a chisel. At that time she knew very little herself. Later she became very good, but that first time when she showed me it was almost as if the blind was leading the blind.

I looked at my first stone. I didn't hesitate. I knew at once it had to become a bird. My childhood torments were tied in with birds: pheasants, pink ibises, ducks, swans. My emotions were linked with their movements.

I decided to make a little bird with his head turned sideways into his body. Quite an ambitious attempt when one has never before cut stone! Once again I was alone, trying something new, searching to express my feelings. It was an exciting challenge: I was like Don Quixote rediscovering the world. While I was working Grisha said, "You're too slow. You're not going about it the right way. When sculptors work, stone flies in all directions."

Nevertheless, I struggled for two years and I finally produced the bird.

Afterward, I saw an exhibition by Anthony Amato in Beverly Hills and was extremely impressed. It seemed that Amato could cut into stone as if it were wax. I wanted to study with him, but he lived in Vista, California, and I was told he was hard to reach. However, Grisha and I drove out to his house and met a young man close to my daughter's age, quite reserved, with a charming wife who spoke even less than he did. He showed me his power tools and even offered to let me try to use the air hammer. We bought a sculpture he had at home, and that made him happy. When Grisha told him I wanted lessons, he refused. "I don't teach," he said. But when Grisha wanted something he knew how to get it. Before Amato realized what hit him, Grisha had talked him into trying to teach me.

When Amato came to Los Angeles, I was very happy with my first lesson. He showed me how to handle the tools and how to cut the stone. He didn't give me flowery dissertations or unnecessary explanations—just straightforward technique. We immediately became friends, and he kept coming back. I was particularly grateful that he didn't speak of art, as I knew in my depths what I wanted to say.

In Ferrières when I was young, my bedroom and the schoolroom had overlooked the lake with ducks of different colors and sizes, and swans, sometimes with their little ones trailing behind them. I spent hours, days, months watching them. Fear, torment, and anxiety were in me then; peace and flowing harmony came to me from the gliding birds. Now as I started to handle the stone with a little more ease, the past seemed to blend with nature, with the fluttering convolutions of ducks

and swans, and the famous poem by Alfred de Musset that I
particularly liked came back to me:

> Lorsque le pélican, lassé d'un long voyage,
> Dans les brouillards du soir retourne à ses roseaux,
> Ses petits affamés courent sur le rivage
> En le voyant au loin s'abattre sur les eaux.
> Déjà, croyant saisir et partager leur proie,
> Ils courent à leur père avec des cris de joie
> En secouant leurs becs sur leurs goîtres hideux.
> Lui, gagnant à pas lents une roche élevée,
> De son aile pendante abritant sa couvée,
> Pêcheur mélancolique, il regarde les cieux.
> Le sang coule à longs flots de sa poitrine ouverte;
> En vain il a des mers fouillé la profondeur;
> L'Océan était vide et la plage déserte;
> Pour toute nourriture il apporte son coeur.
> Sombre et silencieux, étendu sur la pierre,
> Partageant à ses fils ses entrailles de père,
> Dans son amour sublime il berce sa douleur,
> Et, regardant couler sa sanglante mamelle,
> Sur son festin de mort il s'affaisse et chancelle,
> Ivre de volupté, de tendresse et d'horreur
> Mais parfois, au milieu du divin sacrifice,
> Fatigué de mourir dans un trop long supplice,
> Il craint que ses enfants ne le laissent vivant;
> Alors il se soulève, ouvre son aile au vent,
> Et, se frappant le coeur avec un cri sauvage,
> Il pousse dans la nuit un si funèbre adieu,
> Que les oiseaux des mers désertent le rivage,
> Et que le voyageur attardé sur la plage,
> Sentant passer la mort, se recommande à Dieu.

Translated, the poem says: The exhausted pelican returns
home in the evening fog, having found no food for his little
ones. As they see him from afar, landing on the waters, they
run toward him along the shore, shaking their beaks over their
hideous pouches, already with the belief of snatching and sharing their prey. He slowly reaches a high rock. With hanging
wing, melancholy fisherman, he looks at the sky. Blood pours

from his open chest. In vain he plumbed the depths of the seas. The ocean was empty, the beach a desert. For food he brings only his heart. Somber and silent, spread on the stone, sharing with his sons the entrails of their father. In his sublime love he rocks his pain, watching the blood run from his breast. On his feast of death he sinks and staggers, drunk with the pleasure of tenderness and horror. But at times amidst the divine sacrifice, tired of dying in too long a torture, he fears his children will let him live. He rises, opens his wing to the wind, stabbing his heart with a savage shriek. He throws into the night such a funereal adieu that the birds of the sea desert the shore and the traveler lingering on the beach, feeling the passage of death, looks up to God.

Musset's poem was meant as a beautiful metaphor of what the poet gives to the world. He says the great poets are like the pelican as they feed humanity with their own wounds when they speak of deceived hope, of sadness and forgetfulness of love and unhappiness. Their declamations are like swords that trace a blinding circle in the air but from which always hang a few drops of blood.

But when I first read the poem, I was only struck by the bird's despair at failing to find food for his children, and his willingness to feed them with blood from his own heart.

Through the birds, I was expressing myself for the first time. Stone came to life—malleable, tender, sensuous. Sadness came out as I made a dead bird lying on its side, with its head hanging over the base. When I had almost finished I walked out of the studio—to find, right outside the door, a dead sparrow lying on its side. Eerie.

I kept working with the stone for ten years. At first I didn't question results. I was driven from within! I had to do it. Grisha always said, "One does not choose the cello, it chooses one." Maybe the stone had chosen me. Sometimes an old frustration emerged, a negative defeated attitude, a shadow from the past. I would look at my work and say, without any justifiable reason, "It is bad," and suddenly I felt incompetent. But then realistic thinking took over. "Bad! Why is it bad?" I asked myself. "What is bad in that piece—the conception, the construction, the execution? Whatever weakness you feel, name it, name it aloud, work, improve it." And so I did.

Bethsabée, with more ability than I, studied and passed her baccalaureate but didn't continue with the same drive for personal achievement. Instead, she dwelt on promoting others. She eventually moved to Israel where she created and subsidized a very successful dance troupe.

Friends were starting to tell me that I should show my work. I knew it would be difficult, as I had no intention of selling it. I thought that possibly a university would consider an exhibition. I called the University of Southern California, where my husband was a professor. They sent someone to see my work. Six months went by before they told me USC could not show it. That didn't bother me, as I didn't think my work was of a professional level. But I knew it did have my own signature and that for the first time in my life I was able to express myself by letting my inner feelings flow into the stone.

I was working and improving. I was starting to achieve.

Grisha: Our Relationship

Though Grisha's background and my own were opposites, both our ancestors' roots were in the ghetto—Grisha's family in Russia and mine in Frankfurt, Germany, where my great-great-grandfather was a Talmudic student. But while I was raised in luxury, Grisha grew up in poverty. Although it was difficult for him to adjust to the Rothschilds, he was proud to enter a famous family, as I was proud to become the wife of a great artist. As a little boy he had lived through pogroms, hiding underground so as not to be killed, while I, overprotected, was served meals by a footman wearing white gloves. When he was a child, Grisha's daily meals consisted of borscht; in those times his mother often said, "Today the soup is better than yesterday, and will be better still tomorrow." My meals included lobster and pheasant with Château Lafite family wine. Grisha's mother could not read or write; his uncle was a barber. My father was regent of the Bank of France, economically and socially powerful. But when we met, his past and my past were erased. Through my parents I had, in a way, tasted a public life that emerged from luxury and was based on the power of money; now I entered a public life that emerged from the ghetto and was based on talent, work, and self-education.

Grisha's grandfather had a book shop but his son, Pavel (Grisha's father), refused to work in the shop. His dream was music and his ambition was to become a concert violinist. His father forbade him to study violin and threatened to cut off all financial help if he pursued his crazy dream. Pavel could not believe that his father would be that cruel, so he defied him and left for St. Petersburg to study violin with Professor Auer. Grisha's mother remained alone with five young children and no money. When Grisha went to his grandfather for help, he was thrown out.

At that time Grisha was only eight years old. He had been playing cello for a year. So he took his cello and looked for work. He already played so well that in spite of his young age he got a job, first in a night club, which was also a house of prostitution. One of the girls took a liking to the eight-year-old boy and Grisha became jealous of the men who were using her. That situation eventually led the manager to say, "The kid is bad for business," and Grisha lost his job. His next work was in a silent movie house, where every action, every mood had to be illustrated with music. His job was to find and play the proper piece. He was excited by the challenge and says in his book, *Cellist*, "The orchestra, the repertoire, the picture itself I felt were a part of my own creation."

Unfortunately, the conditions were rough in the movie house. He sat in a deep pit where drops of water fell on his head from the new cement on the ceiling. The hours were long for a little boy. On Sundays and holidays he played from three in the afternoon until midnight. When he got so exhausted that he could not play, the conductor screamed and insulted him. Grisha fell into a rage and broke a chair on the conductor's head, and that was the end of his job.

Somehow Grisha's family survived for a year, after which his father returned, and one day Grisha was told that his sister, Nadja, was engaged to the boy Dmitri in the apartment below. His father was pleased and said, "She's not leaving us; she is only moving a few steps down." But Grisha knew Dmitri and his quarreling and hard-drinking parents with whom the young couple would have to live, so he answered his father, "It's not a *few* steps down. It's miles deep into a cesspool." His father reacted with anger, but Grisha had been head of the family while his father was away, so he continued, "Nadja will be maltreated by her husband's drunken parents. Her life will be crippled. She will not thank you, Father, she will hate you and so will I." In his book Grisha writes, "Father's eyes went through me like fire. He struck me and said, 'She *will* marry Dmitri!'" Grisha defied his father by saying "'As long as I am her brother, she will not marry him.'

"'You are no longer her brother. Get out.'"

Grisha took his cello and stepped out in the freezing winter. He was only nine years old. Convinced his mother would call him back, he waited outside his home. But a couple of hours went by and he had no sign from his family. Hanging on to his cello, he slowly walked away, alone in the night. He walked until he lost consciousness but was found and saved by a kind old man, Mr. Shutkin, who nursed his frozen feet and hands. Grisha stayed with Mr. Shutkin, who gave him a table for a bed, and he swore that he would never return home.

Contrary to Grisha's childhood, our relationship was based on a bond of solidity. *I* gave him the much-needed security of a home, and he protected *me*. When, without any reason, residual fear from my childhood reappeared, he said, "As long as I am here nothing bad will ever happen to you," and I believed him.

But living with a famous artist is not easy. Concert tours are not conducive to family life. If I stayed home I seldom saw my husband; if I traveled with him I abandoned the children to strangers. I had to choose: my husband or my children. When I first started traveling I was very uneasy. I wasn't sure how to behave. Grisha was very nervous and tense before each concert and, in order to preserve energy for his appearance, somewhat silent. Meals followed a routine: a fairly substantial lunch and, for dinner, approximately two and one-half hours before the concert, two very soft boiled eggs with tea and toast in his bedroom. As he needed some privacy to rest, we nearly always had adjoining rooms. Blending into his schedule meant a total violation of one's own rhythm of life. Some outsiders would say, "You're so lucky to travel so much and see the world." But in reality I saw only airports, hotel rooms, and concert halls. Whenever Grisha sensed that was not enough for me it made his life more difficult, and I certainly didn't want to add any pressures. Not only was it impossible for me to help, but often I felt that I was in the way. Sometimes, before the concert, he would play a passage twice for me and ask which was better. I didn't hear the difference. He would play again and, ignoring my embarrassment, point out the difference. Then he would say, "Don't worry, the second half of our life will be beautiful. We will have a great second half."

After the concert someone always gave a party. There Grisha was able to release an enormous amount of tension. He would eat and talk, and was happy to be the center of attention. As he started to relax, tension built in me and turned to impatience. During those evenings I waited until finally it was time to go home. We said good-bye, and stood in front of the open door talking for another twenty minutes. Then it was hard to remain polite. So most of the time I stayed home with the children. But then Grisha often complained of how lonely his life was.

The strain and demands of concerts are grueling. Grisha gave all of himself to his art. Though he loved me and his children, he was really married to the cello. Sometimes, however, his artistic power was stifled by its limitations. He would say, out of frustration, "I want it to sound like a trumpet."

He was also tender and softhearted. The shades he deployed in playing brought magic to his phrasing. His sensitivity was so penetrating that he often understood people better than they understood themselves. He seemed to look right through them. That gift led my son-in-law to explain, "He has X-ray eyes."

A newspaper once referred to him as a "gentle giant." Yes, he was both: gentle and big in every respect. His dreams from childhood on were so broad as to encompass the entire world. He liked a painting by Kay Fiel which represented a symbolic portrait of him as a tall man in the foreground, dominating and towering over the world. Music is, after all, the universal language. Though he often said, "I would give my right arm for the family," he really belonged to the world.

Though Grisha and I had much in common, our personalities were quite different. I was shy, afraid of people, and only felt my true self when alone. Grisha was outgoing. He needed to speak; he needed his public. When we went out socially he

loved to entertain with fantastic stories and a tremendous
sense of humor. He talked freely and made his listeners laugh.
His friends, acquaintances, and admirers always gathered
around him while his ideas flowed. While he always found the
right stories to enchant his audience, I felt a little left out.
Sometimes when we got home I asked, "How can you talk so
much?"

"If I hadn't talked, the party would have been dead," he
would tell me.

Of course, that was not the only reason why he spoke so
much. I knew that, for him, talking was a need so that he could
recharge his batteries. One day I became curious to find out
how long he could speak without any encouragement, so I decided to try a little experiment. When we went out to dinner
alone in a restaurant I let him speak and I remained silent. He
was bubbling with ideas, rich in imagination, oozing with free
associations, and he spoke for two and one-half hours. He
needed the outlet, he needed to shine, he needed the public.
Even at home during meals he "entertained" us, sometimes at
the expense of the children relating their school experiences.
So, whether alone or in the family, or with friends and acquaintances like Charlie Chaplin, Aldous Huxley, or George
Burns, he would dominate the conversation. Once, on a ship
late at night, I felt out of it and was tired, so I left him at a
party and went to bed. He joined me a few hours later and
came in quietly, like a child who had done something wrong.
"Are you mad at me?" he asked.

"No, I'm not mad, but what brings out the best in you kills
the best in me." Nothing more was said.

We had our differences and, like all married couples, our
quarrels. But Grisha, the children, and I abided by an important rule: after a quarrel we would never remain angry for
more than ten minutes. So always one of us came and said,
"Do you want to be friends?" and the fight was in the past.

Between us there was a deep understanding on every important matter. Our values were alike: honesty and integrity
above all. We both valued art above material objects, and we
both knew the real value of work. Grisha was world-famous
and needed his success as he needed oxygen to breathe, but

more than this, he knew, and so did I, the value of loving one's activity. As George Burns puts it, "Work only works if the work one is working at is not work." Even though recognition is important, the involvement in one's work is a fulfillment in itself.

I was afraid Grisha would get bored with me as I was uneducated and read very little, but he gave me confidence when he said, "You have a natural intelligence, not spoiled by books. That is more valuable than an education." Through our life he was proud of me, proud when I studied Russian, learned to fly, played competitive chess and tennis, and later when I sculpted. I was proud of him not only because he was a great artist but also because he was intelligent and good-looking and had great judgment, on which I relied. He was wise and kind enough to encourage me to continue my own activities when he went to play cards with friends. When I felt guilty at not accompanying him, he reassured me by saying, "We're not twins."

Though we shared few activities and our interests seemed to pull us apart, the solidity of our marriage came from the quality of our love. Grisha knew that no matter what, I would always love him; he knew that if he lost his fame, if he got disfigured or if he did something wrong, *no matter what*, he could come home to love and understanding, and I knew that was also true for me. What we shared was more than merely being in love. It compared to the best of a good mother's love, because it was unconditional.

[36]

Chess Promotion

At the time I was involved in chess tournaments, Grisha said, "You must do something big—organize an international tournament. It should be called the Piatigorsky Cup. We must get Bobby Fischer and, from Russia, the world champion, Tigran Petrosian." Yes, Grisha was always thinking big. Of course, I knew that would be very costly, but I thought it was a really good idea. There was no important tournament held in the United States. The last international tournament had been held in Dallas in 1957, and the world champion had not been present. We created a chess foundation, not only to promote the Piatigorsky Cup, but to encourage chess in public schools and for underprivileged, crippled, and deaf children.

At one time we were teaching chess in every crippled children's school in and around Los Angeles. I organized a program to teach in schools for deaf children. I even learned a little sign language so as to be able to communicate with them myself. But those schools resented our interference, and when we got there they made it a point to have the children out at a ball game. Although the children loved the game, we were obliged to give up. I organized a club for deaf people, which was successful as long as I was running it, but when I had to go out of town for a while, I found the club had disintegrated so I discontinued it. I worked with the youth center of the public schools to promote tournaments, one of which was called the Tournament of Champions. The idea was to encourage schools to hold a chess tournament during the year. The winner of each school tournament would represent his school in the Tournament of Champions. Another effort was the Christmas tournament held during Christmas vacation. When we started, about 125 children entered. We kept building it up every year until we had over 1,200 children. At that point I thought that, as the tournament was so well liked, the schools' youth center could continue it. I supplied them with the same amount of funds and the same people who had helped me to work for them, and I withdrew. Each year there were fewer entries, until it almost reached the point at which we had started. It was discouraging to have to discontinue the tournament.

The First Piatigorsky Cup, held in 1963, was an international grand master event comprising eight players: from the Soviet Union, Keres and the world champion Petrosian; Najdorf and Panno from Argentina; Gligoric from Yugoslavia; Olafsson from Iceland; and Benko and Reshevsky from the United States.

Though Bobby Fischer was not yet world champion, he was a famous star and probably the greatest player. Naturally, we tried to get him. He wouldn't appear under the same conditions as the other players—he wanted more money. I felt that complying with his demands would lower the standard of the tournament. I was anxious to hold a genuinely high quality event. I was criticized from all sides. People said, "The United States has to be represented by the best player"; "We cannot hold the tournament without Fischer"; "He is a genius; one has to cater to him." Even my husband disapproved of my views. But I held on to what I believed.

Until then, the only way the public could follow the games was by setting up magnetic boards and having youngsters run back and forth, moving pieces on the board to adjust to each new position. It was cumbersome. So I invented a new system with overhead projectors and electric clocks so the public could not only follow the games comfortably, but also the time control.

Three years later, in the Second Piatigorsky Cup, Fischer

played under the same conditions as everyone else. I think I was the first person ever to stand up to him.

The invitations to the Second Piatigorsky Cup went out. Everyone accepted except the Russians. Months went by. We started sending telegrams: silence from Russia. Six months went by before the phone rang from the Soviet Embassy, asking for my husband. As I happened to answer the phone, I could not resist and said, "In Russia they are really not polite."

"What do you mean?" said an indignant voice.

"We invited Petrosian and Keres to play in the Second Cup. We have written and wired and we never got an answer. That is rude."

"Oh, I am sorry," said the voice on the telephone, "you will hear from them right away."

A few days later a telegram came: "Thank you for your invitation." We waited. Another two weeks went by. Another telegram came that said, "Sorry, we are not free on that date." Within the hour I invited two other players. Finally we had eight players. We proceeded with the arrangements—renting the hall, making room reservations, printing the programs, and many other commitments.

A few weeks before the tournament, Grisha went to Moscow as a member of the jury for the Tchaikovsky Competition. After he had been there a few days I received a telegram: "Could you still arrange to include Petrosian and Keres in the tournament?" I was stunned. Was he pressured? Did he want me to say yes? Would he be in any danger if we refused? Prize money would be doubled, rental of the hall should be extended if possible, programs reprinted, publicity changed. I tried to stall, answering that it would be extremely difficult to incorporate Petrosian and Keres and reorganize the tournament, but that I would try. A second telegram came, more insistent, so I finally accepted. During Grisha's stay the players themselves had come to him, so very unhappy, begging him to help them get into the tournament. As I said, it was difficult and very costly; nevertheless, we rearranged the tournament to adjust to ten players. But when I. Kashdan, the chess editor of the *Los Angeles Times* and the director of the tournament, went to meet them on arrival, they weren't on the plane. No message, no explanation. They missed the introductory meeting night and they were not there for the draw. Finally, we heard that their visas had not come through but that they would arrive in time to play. And they did.

Russia dominated the chess world, and still does. With the one exception of Bobby Fischer, who became world champion in 1972, the Russians have been world champions since 1948. But that was not sufficient reason to dictate to the head of the International Federation.

To become world champion, there were four steps. First, each country held a tournament, the Zonal, to determine a representative. Then each representative competed in a large tournament, the Interzonal, and the top six or eight players proceeded with a series of matches by elimination, as in tennis, and the winner of those matches had the right to challenge the world champion.

One of the last semifinal matches was scheduled to be played in Pasadena in 1983 between Korchnoi and Kasparov. Korchnoi had defected, and Kasparov was the very brilliant young Russian threat to Karpov, the world champion. An enormous amount of work and money went into preparing the Pasadena match. When everything was ready, the Russians started warning, "You do not have the proper security; we are not sure Kasparov should come." They kept management and the public hanging on their indecision and at the last minute refused to let him come. So on the scheduled starting date of the tournament Mr. Campomanes, the president of the International Federation, had the board set up. The public was there and, according to the official rules, he started the clock, waited one hour, and then officially forfeited Kasparov in favor of Korchnoi.

The next day Mr. Campomanes came to see me and said, "If we can schedule the start of the final match immediately, my forfeit will be upheld." I was silent. "But we need money; could you help us?"

"How much do you need?"

"A hundred thousand dollars. If we do not get it, the Russians will not accept the forfeit."

Of course I didn't give them a hundred thousand dollars, and the forfeit was ignored. Korchnoi had to play the match when and where the Russians decided. It is true that Korchnoi was asked if he was willing to play and he accepted. I wonder how much choice he really had. Kasparov, after beating Korchnoi, went on to win the world championship title. Why did Russia dictate? The last person courageous and crazy enough to stand up to the Russians was Bobby Fischer. He managed to impose some changes in order to eliminate certain unfairnesses. Why are people so afraid of the Russians?

[37]

A Transfer

As I have already said, for many years I mistook winning for success. Of course winning is part of success. Success is achieving one's goal. But if one's goal is criminal, success is a tragedy. The internal feeling of achievement is a major part of success.

The most common form of accepted success is making or earning a lot of money. Consequently, a person with a lot of money is automatically considered successful, regardless of achievements. Yet many wealthy kids are destroyed by drugs and are in and out of prison. Great wealth often cuts the incentive and changes values from achievements to a desire for objects: wanting to own more jewelry or a Rolls Royce. Many people find it easier to buy than to labor! But do those people ever get a feeling of achievement?

The internal feeling of achievement can be reached in a variety of ways. The way I found came through love.

Success is generally happy and joyful. After the Second World War, my father put in a claim for his home on rue St. Florentin which the Petain government had stolen. But to no avail. From the United States he wrote many letters, but the new government ignored his request. Then he returned to France and tried again. He tried until his last breath. Two months after he died, Talleyrand's palace was returned. Sometimes success can be sad.

How did I emerge from under such a protective boulder? How did the torrent of feelings break through the granite wall? How did a stamped failure become a success? Because I *do* consider myself a success. Should I say that I achieved it in spite of my kennel keepers, or because I was, in spite of myself, soaked in beauty and exposed to various activities? Perhaps it was luck: powerful dynamic genes capable of breaking through any obstacles. Or maybe those very obstacles made me fight and become strong. Yes, partly.

I was big and yet so small. Because I was insecure and shy, people saw me only as a Rothschild and decided that I was cold and snobbish. I was a Rothschild, so a "success," but seemingly I did not live up to my position. I was a disappointment. There were no demands on me, and yet expectations. People pointed at me, admired, and envied. Rothschild: the world is open—open to a shrinking, misunderstood child. But in me there was hidden anger with internal explosions, and, contrary to the judgment of many, I emerged because of the power of love which flowed from me and was given back to me by Grisha, Jephta, and Joram.

Because I started my life as a failure, I could not see that I was born in a privileged situation. But through the years I tasted the best of two worlds: the world of luxury and the world of art. I did not appreciate belonging to an outstanding family—daring, generous, and of great integrity. I had suffered and I wanted to go forward, away from Rothschild. I met a cellist and became part of *his* glory. I transferred from material richness to the richness of art and to real richness, human richness. "Kneel to the rising sun!" Yes, I did emerge—I am a Piatigorsky.

Now darkness was seeping into our lives. Though Grisha was still concertizing and teaching, he was tired, anxious, tormented, worried, creating problems to the point of self-destruction.

He said over and over again: "I hate concerts, I hate the profession; we will have a good second life." He suffered, but he could not survive without the stage, without his public.

After sixty years of smoking, he had emphysema and chronic

bronchitis. Plagued with hemorrhoids, he would complain, "I am so tired. I just want to be left alone." But he could not accept the peace of mind he longed for. When he slowed down it was painful for him to see others go ahead. He craved to play, and the harder it became the stronger he hung on. Not playing meant death. When he tried to explain he said, "It is like cats scratching my insides."

To his students he gave all of himself. When they came early in the morning I asked, "Will they be here for lunch?" "No," he said. But they were still there for dinner. He was hanging on. He wanted to live, while at the same time he was torturing and destroying himself. To try to forget his worries every morning he lost himself in the study of the stock market. Buying and selling stocks challenged him and became a daily game.

Television was also one of his few relaxations. I often found him watching wrestlers and practicing cello at the same time, mostly the left hand only with no sound. During those years I kept working with stone, and Grisha always helped me, taking an interest, encouraging, giving intelligent and constructive criticisms. He also enjoyed cards, and from time to time went in the evenings to friends to play bridge or gin rummy while I stayed home and worked in the studio. I was consolidating as he was going down, and as if to cheer himself he would say once again, "the second half of our lives—the second half—"

In 1972 we drove to Palm Springs for a few days, hoping to relax; but can one ever run away from oneself? Breaking our habit of sleeping separately, one evening I offered to share a room and he accepted: he had a premonition. In the emptiness of the desert, in a small motel with a telephone only in the main office, I was hoping for a pleasant relief. But he tortured himself with worries and anxiety. That night he fainted on the way to the bathroom because he was bleeding internally. After a few days in an atrocious desert hospital he was able to be moved to UCLA by ambulance and to get proper care. After innumerable tests, the doctors were still unable to find the cause of the internal bleeding.

Then, a couple of years later, his cough was so bad that every morning it took him infinite time to clear his chest before sitting at his desk for breakfast, colorless, tired—so tired, but still indulging in a romance with the stock market.

Then he went for his yearly chest X ray, only to hear that he was sentenced. The X ray showed a tumor. He needed surgery, lung surgery.

Grisha was tender and weak. He could not bear to see people suffer; he also could not handle his own emotions when they were painful, but he could face and withstand physical pain to a frightening degree.

Some years earlier, in Elizabethtown, he had slipped on a pile of broken wood and had injured his thumb. Not realizing it was fractured, and in spite of the pain, he did not hesitate to go and play the next concert. But holding the bow was so painful that tears rolled down his cheeks. The public mistook those tears for an emotional expression of the music, and soon the whole audience was crying.

In 1953 when I was undergoing abdominal surgery for the removal of an ovary, he went through oral surgery, and thinking of me, he said he hardly noticed the drilling, cutting, and bleeding. From the dentist he came straight to the hospital and sat in my room until I was fully conscious. Years later he underwent successful lung surgery. After removing one third of his lung the doctors found no evidence of cancer spreading to the lymph nodes. But we still had heavy hearts.

Eventually he came home; and his first interest was the cello. He got it out and played a few notes, looking at me with a certain shyness and a sad smile. "It can still sing," he said in a low voice.

After those few notes he did not play cello for a year. Suddenly the conductor of the Utah Symphony, Abravanel, called and asked, "Can you play the Dvorak Concerto this weekend?" Grisha looked at me with his hand over the receiver and said, "They want me to play in a few days."

"You have not played in a year."

He hesitated for a minute and accepted. Only a year after his surgery, and now only three days to "warm up"! Oh, but to play again, live, defy sickness! His immense courage gave him the will to live. We went to Salt Lake City. The effort was supreme; defying death, he would come out and make the cello sing. But as he dressed for the concert, he called me. "I cannot button the collar of my shirt. It's too tight." His neck had swollen to twice its size. Breathing was difficult, but nothing could stop him. He came out and played, and he *did* make the cello sing.

Upon our return to Los Angeles after the concert, he reentered the hospital and in one more attempt to fight the recurring cancer underwent radiation treatment. The radiation gave him some relief. Toward the end of the treatment, in April 1976, USC hosted a large celebration for his seventy-third birthday. When he got up for his talk he was still able to joke about himself. He referred to the Piatigorsky Chair USC had created for him as "the wheelchair." Both Jephta and Joram came from the east coast and we were all four reunited for the last time.

After the radiation Grisha was feeling better and it was important for him to return to normal life. He accepted a concert for the following month and he insisted that I go on with my activities as usual. So, in May 1976, we held a charity tennis tournament in the garden, as we had done every year, as a pleasant social day to help the John Tracy Clinic. During the tournament one of the players came to me and said, "I hear you sculpt. I would love to see some of your work." I took him into the studio. He seemed surprised and was full of compliments. "I am an art dealer," he said, "I have my own gallery. I think you should exhibit."

"Oh, that would be nice," I said, "but it would be difficult because I don't want to sell." I knew my husband would not agree to part with the few pieces I had.

"Well, I think that can be arranged."

We made an appointment to go to his gallery and talk. Grisha was barely over the radiation treatment. He was tired and sick, but he came with me to the gallery. We were punctual for the appointment, and we waited. The owner didn't show up. Finally someone from the gallery came to us and said, "Mr.———is sorry but he will not be able to be here; I can replace him and make arrangements for your exhibition."

Such disrespect was certainly not an inducement. "Let's forget it," I suggested.

Grisha had a musician friend in Beverly Hills who had a gallery that was going very well. When Grisha called him he said, "Oh no, you don't want to go to Mr.————. He doesn't have a good reputation, but I will be happy to give your wife an exhibition. She doesn't have to sell. You have been a friend to me; it is my luck to be able to do something for you."

Grisha was so very sick, and yet he was helping me. Life was leaving him, and he was injecting life into me!

[38]

Recognition

M y exhibition, the tangible expression of my transfer to the world of art, was set for early October, five months ahead. Would Grisha be there?

With immense courage he went to Philadelphia and played the Brahms Double Concerto with Isaac Stern and Eugene Ormandy conducting at the Robin Hood Dell. He could barely walk a block, but he got out in front of several thousand people and played beautifully. From there we went to Zurich, Switzerland, where he taught a summer course for several weeks in July. His old friend, Milstein, was teaching the violin classes. Grisha stayed eight to ten hours every day in a smoke-filled, crowded room, listening to students, explaining and encouraging. At the end of the day he lay on the bed with a fever and coughing up blood, but he would *not* give up. I waited and watched, convinced we would never make it home. But when it came time to leave, we took the Concorde from Paris to Washington and stayed forty-eight hours in my son's house, and we did make it back to Los Angeles. At the airport Grisha was too weak to walk, so I took his cello and pushed him in his wheelchair to a taxi.

Grisha died a couple of weeks later, on August 6, 1976.

Shortly afterward Mr. Ed Acosta of the Acosta gallery called to schedule the opening date for the exhibition of my sculptures. I didn't think I could go through with the show, but my children both said, "You have to! Father arranged it and would be very upset if you didn't." Grisha's doctor and our friend, Lailee Bakhtiar, also insisted that I go through with plans for the exhibition. So with great help from my children I agreed to go ahead.

Grisha had set it up though he was not there to see it. His death was a great loss to his students and many of his friends, so they all came to my exhibition as a tribute to him.

I think it was well viewed and also stood on its own two feet. One day I got a call from a friend saying that the mayor of Beverly Hills wanted to buy a large piece, two birds intertwined, which I called "Fusion." The gallery told her it was not for sale. She had saved nine thousand dollars to donate an art work to city hall for the center of their large entrance and had been looking for something for a long time. Would I please change my mind? That was a very flattering offer and a lot of money for a totally unknown sculptor.

Then I remembered an incident of my youth. I was then still married to Calmann-Levy. We had rented a house at the seashore and his brother, Pierre, was spending the summer with us. The two brothers went out. I was practicing the piano in the downstairs living room with an open window overlooking the ocean when some boisterous kids went by and threw a couple of pennies through the open window. I didn't know whether or not it was a joke, but I picked up the pennies, smiled and said aloud, "I just earned my first money," and wondered if I would ever earn any more!

In city hall my piece would not be lost. I agreed to sell it with the stipulation that the day they no longer wanted it, my children would have the option to buy it back for the same price I had sold it for.

Then to help fill the emptiness of living alone I got a tiny puppy. My new little friend was a Boston terrier named Musty.

I continued sculpting and played tennis regularly twice a week. Eventually I entered senior tournaments, often reaching the finals in the nationals, which meant getting a silver ball. Winning and getting a gold ball seemed out of reach. But as I kept improving, a top player asked me to play doubles with her, and we won. My first gold ball was a thrill.

A couple of years later in the same tournament, while helping a lady move a table the day before my semifinals singles match, I slipped and hit my chest. I heard a crack and felt a sharp pain. That night I couldn't turn in bed and the next morning struggled a long time before I was able to get up. In spite of pain, I played my semifinal match. I won the first set and lost the second, at which time I went to my coach and said, "I can't continue, I am in an agony of pain." He looked at me and said, "You are not going to let that little squirt win?" He was anxious for me to succeed and knew how to spur me on. So I went back on the court and, despite the pain which made me a shadow of myself, won the third set six-love. I defaulted the finals but still won the doubles, thanks to my strong partner. When I got home the X ray showed a sizable fracture of the chest bone. So in spite of a bone fracture I had won a silver and a gold ball.

After that I didn't play for six weeks. I asked the doctor when I would be able to start playing again. He answered, "When you can turn in bed."

Once at a dinner, a very old friend of my husband embarrassed me with a compliment. "She flew a plane, she is a chess champion, a tennis champion, a sculptor . . ." and, lifting his glass toward me, he said, "a toast to Jacqueline." I smiled but shriveled inside. I had never won the United States chess championship. I had never won a gold ball in singles. I had got involved in a variety of things, and I knew that I could not really become good at anything. I was a success in other people's eyes, not in my own.

But what would it mean to me to be a success? Getting an extra title and the adulation strewn upon winners? Would that make up for the love I didn't get when I was very young? Was any success of mine still searching for my mother's admiration? Or did it mean being at peace with myself, accepting myself as I really was? Maybe success is the physical satisfaction of striving, or the joy one helps to spread to one's surroundings. When my puppy chases a rubber toy I throw, brings it to my feet, panting and wagging her tail, jumping up and licking my face, is that not also success? Sometimes people who have received much recognition don't feel successful, whereas others do who haven't received recognition. What really matters is one's inner feeling.

After my husband had died, I saw a friend, who had been United States chess champion many times. As we were talking at dinner, I remembered meeting her in New York in the final game of the National Championship. I was in the lead; a draw would have given me the title. I developed a good game, a combinative game, and finally I saw what I thought was a winning move. I got so nervous and so excited that all the pieces were dancing before my eyes. Was I wrong? I tried to go over the variation. The clock was running; if I waited too long, time would run out. I still thought that move would win, but I did not trust myself. Winning was too good to be true. As the British say, "She does not have the stomach to win." I glanced at my opponent, who had been U.S. champion for the last six years. Imposing. She almost smiled. Fear—yes, fear still was the story of my life! I saw my time getting shorter; I looked for security, froze, made a different move which I thought would be safer—and lost, ending second, half a point behind the champion. As we were talking at dinner, I said, "I was surprised, after my husband died, to see how many friends I had."

"And I," she said, "was surprised to see how many friends I did not have." I wondered which of us was more successful. Had I been mistaking winning for success?

Once I heard a young woman affirming her success in everything she did. Now she wanted to write, but she didn't. She kept saying, "What I really want to do is write." When a friend asked, "But why don't you?" she answered, "I'm afraid to fail. I have never failed." I suppose she forgot that, as they say in the boxing world, "Success comes to he who knows how to get up off the ground." If you are afraid of a dog, he will attack you, but if you face him with outstretched hands he will, in most cases, sniff and make friends.

Defy fear; it will hide and shrink. Hit fear head on; it will crumble like the glass door my childhood friend Colette crashed through when challenged. To overcome one's weakness is success.

Fear? No more. Fear *was* the story of my life.

Both my children are superior people. My daughter is beautiful, my son extremely good-looking, both of them highly intelligent, genuine, kind. That is success, real success. Jephta and Joram chose wonderful human beings for their spouses. Furthermore, their qualities have carried through to the next generation. I am happy and proud to say that my five grandsons are also superior human beings.

One of my grandsons, Eric, wrote a paper in high school on a person who had been somewhat influential in his life. I was stunned when I heard that he had written about me and had referred to me as a winner.

My mother had said when I was young and struggling, "I wish I had a child that could also win, but . . ."

I may have lost many times, but I *am* a winner.